BARCELONA GUIDE BOC__

A Detailed Travel Guide to Immerse Yourself in History, Arts & Culture to See Iconic Landmarks, Hidden Gems, Affordable Lodging & Dining, Easy City Navigation & Much More

NICHOLAS INGRAM
NÚRIA BRUGUERA

All rights reserved © 2023 **Nicholas Ingram**

No part of this publication may be reproduced, distributed, or transmitted in any form or by any means, including photocopying, recording, or other electronic or mechanical methods, without the prior written permission of the publisher, except in the case of brief quotations embodied in critical reviews and certain other noncommercial uses permitted by copyright law. For permission requests, contact: theworldexplorergs@gmail.com

PARK GUELL

CONTENTS

INTRODUCTION	1
History, Geography and Weather of Barcelona	4
Why You Should Visit Barcelona	7
CHAPTER 1: PLANNING YOUR TRIP	9
Things You Should Know Before You Go	10
Best Time to Visit Barcelona	12
How to Get to Barcelona	14
Getting Around Barcelona	15
CHAPTER 2: EXPLORING BARCELONA	21
THE 10 DISTRICTS OF BARCELONA	22
TOP 12 MUST-SEE NEIGHBOURHOODS OF BARCELONA	24
TOP 17 MUST-SEE LANDMARKS AND ATTRACTIONS IN BARCELONA	38
Basilica of the Sagrada Familia	39
Park Güell	41
La Pedrera - Casa Milà	43
Casa Batlló	45
Mercado de La Boqueria	47
Palau de la Música Catalana	49
Camp Nou - FC Barcelona's Iconic Stadium	51
Cathedral of Barcelona	53
Mount Tibidabo	55
Magic Fountain of Montjuïc	57

Basilica of Santa Maria del Mar	59
Picasso Museum	61
Güell Palace	63
Ciutadella Park	65
Plaça de Catalunya	67
Casa Vicens Gaudí	69
14 LESSER-KNOWN PLACES & UNDER-THE-RADAR GEMS IN BARCELONA	71
TOP 8 MUST-VISIT MUSEUMS IN BARCELONA	79
CosmoCaixa	81
Erotic Museum of Barcelona (Museu de l'Erotica)	83
Parc de Montjuic	85
Joan Miro Foundation	87
Museu d'Historia de Barcelona - MUHBA	89
Museu Maritim de Barcelona	91
Museo Egipci de Barcelona	93
20 MORE MUSEUMS IN BARCELONA YOU MIGHT CONSIDER VISITING	95
VIBRANT FESTIVALS AND EVENTS TO SEE WHILE YOU'RE IN BARCELONA	98
THE BEACHES OF BARCELONA	100
CHAPTER 3: BARCELONA DINING AND CULINARY DELIGHTS	103
16 Catalan Delicacies to Sample in Barcelona	104
10 Budget-Friendly Restaurants and Cafes	107
7 Mid-Range Restaurants in Barcelona	112
5 Fine Dining Restaurants in Barcelona	117
Street Food and Markets in Barcelona	121
Dietary Preferences and Restrictions	122

CHAPTER 4: ACCOMMODATIONS	124
Choosing the Right Accommodation	125
Accommodation Options	126
6 Best Budget Friendly Lodging Recommendation in Barcelona	127
5 Best Mid-Range Lodging Recommendation	132
5 Best Luxury Lodging Recommendation	138
CHAPTER 5: BARCELONA'S NIGHTLIFE & ENTERTAINMENT SCENE	143
9 Best Places To Visit For A Night Out In Barcelona	144
9 Night Activities To Indulge In While In Barcelona	147
CHAPTER 6: SHOPPING AND SOUVENIRS IN BARCELONA	150
Shopping Districts and Streets	151
Local Crafts and Artisans	152
Where to Find Unique Souvenirs	153
CHAPTER 7: BEYOND BARCELONA: TOP 10 DAY TRIPS FROM BARCELONA	154
MONTSERRAT	155
COLLSEROLA	157
GIRONA	159
FIGUERES	161
SITGES	163
VILANOVA I LA GELTRU	165
TARRAGONA	167
MONT BLANC	169
COLÒNIA GÜELL	171
VIC	173
SOME BEAUTIFUL MEDIEVAL VILLAGES IN CATALONIA YOU MIGHT CONSIDER VISITING	175

CHAPTER 8: ITINERARIES	177
5-Hours Barcelona Itinerary	178
1-Day Barcelona Itinerary	180
2-Days Barcelona Itinerary	182
5-Days Itinerary in Barcelona	184
7-Days Itinerary Option 1	185
7-Days Itinerary Option 2	187
CHAPTER 9: PRACTICAL RESOURCES ABOUT BARCELONA	189
Visa Information and Requirements	190
Basics Useful Phrases in Both Catalonian and Spanish	192
Ensuring Safety and Well-being in Barcelona	195
Medical Assistance	197
Contacting the Local Police (Mossos d'Esquadra)	199
Recommended Travel Apps and Websites	200
Recommended Useful Websites	202
MAPS	204
MAP 1: DISTRICTS OF BARCELONA	205
MAP 2: THE HARBOR AND CENTRAL AREA OF BARCELONA	206
MAP 3: A MORE DETAILED MAP OF BARCELONA	207
MAP 4: BARCELONA METRO MAP	208
MAP 5: PRINTABLE TOURIST MAP SHOWING THE MAIN ATTRACTIONS OF BARCELONA	209
MAP 6: NEIGHBORHOOD OF BARCELONA	210
MAP 7: LA RAMBLA PEDESTRIAN AVENUE	211
MAP 8: BARCELONA TOP 20 DESTINATIONS	212
MAP 9: BARCELONA TRAMWAY MAP	213
CONLUSION	214

INTRODUCTION

In the heart of Catalonia, beneath the azure skies and kissed by the Mediterranean breeze, lies a city that has danced through the centuries, weaving an intricate tapestry of history, culture, and vibrant life. Welcome to Barcelona, a city that bears witness to the passage of time like few others. As you embark on a journey through its enchanting streets, allow me to share with you a glimpse of its captivating past, a tale that will kindle your curiosity and beckon you to uncover the secrets it holds.

Long before the bustling metropolis we know today, Barcelona was a modest Roman settlement known as Barcino. The very stones upon which you tread bear the imprints of its early inhabitants' dreams and aspirations. Picture the bustling marketplace of ancient Barcino, where merchants from across the Mediterranean converged to trade exotic goods and ideas. Here, the scent of spices mingled with the salty tang of sea air, creating an atmosphere of cosmopolitan allure that endures to this day.

As the Roman era gave way to the Middle Ages, Barcelona experienced a transformation that would shape its destiny for centuries to come. It was during this time that one of the most memorable events in the city's history unfolded—the coronation of Wilfred the Hairy in 878 AD. Legend has it that as he knelt to be anointed, a stroke of destiny occurred. Wilfred raised his hand, revealing fingers stained with the royal blood of a wild boar he had slain in battle. Thus, the royal house of Catalonia was symbolically born, marking the dawn of an era of resilience, creativity, and fervent identity.

But it was in the 19th century that Barcelona truly came into its own, embracing an industrial revolution that propelled it into the modern age. The city buzzed with progress, its streets a stage for innovation, culture, and political fervor. Amidst this backdrop, the remarkable architect Antoni Gaudí etched his indelible mark upon the city's landscape. His masterpieces, including the Sagrada Família and Casa Batlló, stand as testament to a visionary mind that blended nature's forms with human ingenuity, birthing a unique architectural language that Barcelona wears as a crown.

Barcelona experienced both success and challenges throughout the 20th century. The 1992 Summer Olympics marked a spectacular resurgence, showcasing Barcelona's ability to evolve while retaining its soul. The Olympic Games transformed derelict industrial zones into vibrant venues and rekindled the world's fascination with this charismatic city by the sea.

And so, dear reader, as you stand on the crossroads of Barcelona's past and present, you hold within your hands the key to a treasure trove of stories, each stone and street corner a whisper of a bygone era. In the pages that follow, we will traverse the labyrinthine streets of the Gothic Quarter, marvel at the modernist wonders, savor the culinary delights, and immerse ourselves in the vibrant festivals that are woven into the very fabric of this enchanting city.

Barcelona beckons—the allure of its history, the charisma of its people, and the mysteries of its past await your exploration. With every step you take, the city's echoes will speak to you, drawing you deeper into its narrative. So join me, as we peel back the layers of time and unveil the soul of Barcelona, a city that holds the key to its past and a promise of new adventures yet to come.

HISTORY, GEOGRAPHY AND WEATHER OF BARCELONA

HISTORY

Barcelona is a city with a rich and diverse history that dates back to ancient times. It was founded as a Roman city called "Barcino" in the 1st century BC. Over the centuries, it became a significant trading and cultural hub in the Mediterranean region. Barcelona has experienced various rulers and influences, including Visigothic, Moorish, and Frankish rule.

One of the most notable periods in Barcelona's history was during the Middle Ages when it was a part of the Crown of Aragon. During this time, the city played a pivotal role in maritime trade and exploration, which contributed to its prosperity. The Gothic Quarter of Barcelona still reflects the architectural and cultural remnants of this era.

In the late 19th and early 20th centuries, Barcelona underwent significant industrialization and urban expansion. The city became a center of modernist architecture, led by the famous architect Antoni Gaudí, whose masterpieces like the Sagrada Família and Park Güell have become iconic symbols of the city.

In the 20th century, Barcelona faced political upheavals, including the Spanish Civil War and the Franco regime. After Franco's death in 1975, the city experienced a resurgence of cultural and political vitality, contributing to its current status as one of Europe's most dynamic and cosmopolitan cities.

GEOGRAPHY

Barcelona is located in the northeastern part of Spain, on the coast of the Mediterranean Sea. It is both the capital and the largest city in the Catalonia region The city is bordered by the Collserola mountain range to the west, which offers picturesque views of the surrounding area.

The city's geography is characterized by its coastline, which includes several beaches that are popular among both locals and tourists. Barcelona's port has been historically important for trade and transportation.

WEATHER

Barcelona has a Mediterranean climate, which means mild, wet winters and hot, dry summers. Here's a general overview of the weather throughout the year:

Spring (March to May): Spring in Barcelona is mild and pleasant, with temperatures gradually warming up. It's a popular time for tourists, as the weather is comfortable and there's relatively less rainfall.

Summer (June to August): Summers in Barcelona are hot and dry, with average high temperatures reaching the mid-80s to low 90s Fahrenheit (around 30-35°C). It's a peak tourist season due to the warm beach weather and various cultural events.

Autumn (September to November): Autumn remains pleasant, with temperatures gradually cooling down. September is often warm and enjoyable. October and November might see more rainfall, but it's still a good time to visit.

Winter (December to February): Winters in Barcelona are mild compared to many other European cities, with average highs around 50-60°F (10-15°C). While it's the wettest season, the city rarely experiences extreme cold.

Keep in mind that these are general weather patterns, and there can be variations from year to year.

WHY YOU SHOULD VISIT BARCELONA

Barcelona offers a unique blend of history, art, and culture, making it an irresistible destination for travelers. Here are some compelling reasons why you should visit Barcelona:

1. Architectural Marvels: Barcelona is home to some of the world's most breathtaking architecture. From Gaudí's masterpieces to the Gothic Quarter's medieval buildings, the city is a treasure trove of architectural wonders.

2. Artistic Heritage: Barcelona is a haven for art enthusiasts, with world-class museums like the Picasso Museum and MACBA showcasing the city's artistic heritage. The city's vibrant art scene is also evident in its numerous galleries and street art.

3. Culinary Delights: Barcelona is a food lover's paradise, with its diverse culinary scene. From traditional tapas bars to Michelin-starred restaurants, the city offers a wide range of gastronomic experiences.

4. Vibrant Culture and Festivals: Barcelona is known for its vibrant culture and lively festivals. From the colorful celebrations of La Mercè to the electronic music extravaganza of Sonar Festival, there's always something happening in the city.

5. Outdoor Adventures: Barcelona offers a wealth of outdoor activities, from strolling through its parks and relaxing on its beautiful beaches to hiking in the nearby mountains. The moderate weather in the city makes it a perfect choice for those who enjoy outdoor activities.

6. Shopping and Fashion: Barcelona is a shopper's paradise, with its wide range of boutiques, markets, and designer stores. Whether you're looking for unique souvenirs or the latest fashion trends, the city has it all.

7. *Nightlife and Entertainment:* Barcelona has a vibrant nightlife scene, with a wide range of bars, clubs, and live music venues. Whether you're looking for a relaxed evening at a beachfront bar or a night of dancing at a trendy club, Barcelona has something for everyone.

8. *Beaches and Mediterranean Lifestyle:* Barcelona's location on the Mediterranean coast gives it a unique charm. The city's beautiful beaches and relaxed atmosphere make it the perfect destination for those seeking a beach getaway.

CHAPTER 1: PLANNING YOUR TRIP

CHAPTER ONE
PLANNING YOUR TRIP

Barcelona is a city that offers something for every traveler, whether you're seeking cultural immersion, culinary delights, or outdoor adventures. In this chapter, we'll guide you through the essential aspects of planning your trip to Barcelona, including important information you should know about Barcelona, the best time to visit, how to get to the city, and the best way to easily navigate the city of counts.

THINGS YOU SHOULD KNOW BEFORE YOU GO

Catalan Nationalism: The topic of Catalan nationalism is sensitive in Barcelona. To foster harmony, it's wise to refrain from making political statements concerning Catalan independence.

Public Displays of Affection: Demonstrations of public affection are less common in Barcelona compared to some other cultures. To align with local norms, it's advisable to avoid hugging or kissing in public.

Time Zone: Central European Standard Time (CET)

Dining times in Barcelona tend to lean towards the later side. Typically, restaurants open for lunch between 1:30 p.m. and 4:00 p.m., while dinner service runs from 8:30 p.m. to 11:00 p.m. Many shops observe a midday siesta closure (from 2:00 p.m. to 5:00 p.m.), along with closures on Sundays and public holidays.

Camp Nou, situated in Barcelona, claims the title of Europe's largest stadium, boasting a capacity exceeding 99,000 attendees. This iconic venue serves as the home of FC Barcelona, one of the most passionately supported football teams across the globe.

Greetings: When meeting someone in Barcelona, the customary greeting involves a handshake. In more formal situations, opting for the formal "usted" instead of the informal "tu" is advisable.

Punctuality: Unlike in some other countries, punctuality isn't a top priority in Spain. It's not unusual for people to arrive 15-30 minutes late for social gatherings.

Tipping: While not obligatory, leaving a tip in Barcelona is a gesture of appreciation. A small amount of a few euros is generally sufficient.

Dining: Barcelona's meal times adhere to a different schedule than some other places. Lunch is typically enjoyed between 2 pm and 4 pm, while dinner is commonly served from 9 pm to 11 pm.

TIPS FOR MAINTAINING CULTURAL APPROPRIATENESS IN BARCELONA

Dressing modestly is recommended: **Refrain from wearing revealing attire like shorts or tank tops.**

Demonstrate consideration for personal boundaries by keeping a respectful distance from others.

- Acknowledge and respect religious beliefs. **Given Barcelona's diversity and significant Muslim population, consider adhering to religious practices and dress codes.**

- Learning a few basic Spanish phrases demonstrates your respect for the local culture.

BEST TIME TO VISIT BARCELONA

Barcelona enjoys a Mediterranean climate, with mild winters and hot summers. The best time to visit depends on your preferences and what you want to experience in the city.

Factors to weigh when determining the best time to visit Barcelona include:

Weather: Opt for the summer months for warm, sun-soaked days or the shoulder seasons and winter for milder conditions.
Crowds: While summer is bustling, the shoulder seasons and winter promise a quieter experience.
Prices: Costs are highest in summer and lowest in winter.
Events: Barcelona hosts numerous festivals and events throughout the year, so align your visit to match your interests.

The best time to visit Barcelona falls within the shoulder seasons, spanning from *March to May* and *September to October*. During these intervals, the climate remains mild and sunny, with temperatures ranging from 60°F to 80°F (15°C to 27°C). This time offers fewer crowds than the peak summer months, and costs are generally lower.

The summer months *(June to August)* also draw a considerable number of visitors, although they bring with them hot and humid conditions, with temperatures frequently climbing to the high 80s or low 90s (30°C to 32°C). This season can witness significant congestion in the city.

The winter season *(November to February)* features colder weather, with average temperatures spanning from 40°F to 50°F (4°C to 10°C). Occasional rain or snowfall might also occur. However, the city experiences notably fewer tourists during this period, leading to lower prices.

Irrespective of the chosen time, a fulfilling experience awaits you in Barcelona because of its diverse range of attractions, from renowned architecture to stunning beaches and lively nightlife.

HOW TO GET TO BARCELONA

Barcelona is well-connected to major cities around the world, making it easily accessible for travelers. Here are the main transportation options to consider when planning your trip:

1. By Air: Barcelona-El Prat Airport (BCN) is the city's main international airport, located approximately 12 kilometers southwest of the city center. It serves as a hub for both domestic and international flights. From the airport, you can reach the city center by taxi, airport shuttle bus, or train.

2. By Train: Barcelona is well-connected to major cities in Europe by train. The city boasts multiple train stations, with *Barcelona Sants* serving as the primary one. High-speed trains, such as the AVE, provide fast and convenient connections to other Spanish cities, as well as neighboring countries.

3. By Bus: Barcelona has a comprehensive bus network, with several international bus companies operating routes to and from the city. The main bus station is Estació del Nord, located near the city center. Buses offer a more budget-friendly option for traveling to Barcelona.

4. By Car: If you prefer to drive, Barcelona is easily accessible by car. The city is well-connected to major highways, and there are several car rental companies available at the airport and throughout the city. However, be aware that parking in the city center can be challenging and expensive.

GETTING AROUND BARCELONA

Barcelona is a vibrant city with a well-developed public transportation system that makes it easy to navigate and explore. In this chapter, we'll guide you through the various transportation options available in Barcelona, from the efficient metro system to buses, trams, taxis, and ride-sharing services. We'll also provide tips and advice to help you navigate the city with ease.

Public Transportation Options

1. Metro: The TMB (Transports Metropolitans de Barcelona) is Barcelona's main public transportation network, covering the metro and buses. It's a highly efficient way to navigate the city, with numerous lines reaching key attractions and neighborhoods. The metro operates from 5:00 am to midnight (extended on weekends). Tickets can be bought at stations or via the TMB app. A one-way ticket costs €2.40, or you can opt for the T-Casual ticket for multiple trips and better value.

2. Bus: Barcelona's comprehensive bus network spans the city and suburbs, ideal for areas beyond the metro's reach. Well-marked stops and electronic displays indicating stops enhance convenience. Tickets can be obtained on board or via TMB app. Plan around traffic for optimal travel, especially avoiding peak hours.

3. Train: Barcelona's central railway hub is Barcelona Sants station. Extending beyond the city, the FGC (Ferrocarrils de la Generalitat de Catalunya) operates a comprehensive train network that links Barcelona to its suburban regions and neighboring towns within Catalonia. For international connectivity, the _Renfe_ offers a high-speed rail connection spanning Spain and France. This efficient route provides expedient access to cities such as Paris, Marseille, and Madrid.

4. Tram: Barcelona has a modern tram system that serves several neighborhoods, including areas near the beach. The trams are a scenic and leisurely way to travel, offering panoramic views of the city. Like the metro and bus, tickets can be purchased at the stations or through the TMB app.

TIPS FOR NAVIGATING THE CITY USING PUBLIC TRANSPORTATION

1. Plan your route: Before setting out, it's helpful to plan your route using a map or a journey planner app. This will save you time and ensure that you reach your destination efficiently. The TMB app is a useful tool for checking routes, timetables, and ticket information.

2. Validate your ticket: Make sure to validate your ticket when using public transportation in Barcelona. Most tickets need to be validated by tapping them on the card readers located at the entrance of metro stations or on board buses and trams. If a ticket inspector checks your ticket and it hasn't been validated, you may incur a fine.

3. Keep an eye on your belongings: As with any major city, it's important to be mindful of your belongings when using public transportation. Keep your bags and valuables close to you and be aware of your surroundings, especially in crowded areas.

TAXIS AND RIDE-SHARING SERVICES IN BARCELONA

1. Taxis: Taxis are readily available in Barcelona and can be hailed on the street or found at designated taxi ranks. They are a convenient option for short distances or when you have heavy luggage. Taxis in Barcelona are metered, and it's advisable to ask for a receipt at the end of your journey. While tipping is not obligatory, it is welcomed as a gesture of appreciation for excellent service.

2. Ride-sharing services: Barcelona also has ride-sharing services such as Uber and Cabify, which offer an alternative to traditional taxis. These services can be booked through their respective apps, and the fares are usually lower than those of regular taxis. It's important to note that ride-sharing services operate within certain regulations in Barcelona, so it's advisable to familiarize yourself with the rules and requirements before using them.

RENTING A CAR IN BARCELONA (IF APPLICABLE)

Should You Rent a Car?
Making the decision to rent a car depends on weighing the pros and cons:

Pros
Freedom: Allows exploration of the city and its surroundings at your own pace.
Cost Savings: Saves money on organized tours.

Cons

Traffic: Possibility of getting stuck in traffic.

Parking Challenges: Finding parking can be difficult, especially in the city center.

Renting a car in Barcelona offers a sense of liberation, particularly if you plan to venture beyond the city. It's an excellent way to embark on day trips and explore neighboring areas without constraints imposed by public transportation schedules.

REQUIREMENTS TO RENT A CAR IN BARCELONA

Driver's License: A valid driving license, held for at least one year, is necessary.

Additional License: Depending on your country of issue, an International Driver's License might be required.

Proof of Address: Proof of address might be requested, such as a utility bill or rental agreement.

Credit/Debit Card: A valid credit or debit card is needed for payment and security.

Age: The minimum age to rent a car in most cases is 21, though costs might be higher for drivers under 25.

Insurance Requirements: Third-party insurance and a damage waiver are legally required in Spain for rental cars. It's essential to understand your coverage and policy before booking. Collision insurance packages can be added to your reservation.

CHOOSING A CAR

Barcelona offers a range of car types to suit your needs. Compact cars are ideal for narrow streets, while medium-sized cars provide more comfort for families. Premium cars like BMW and

Mercedes can be chosen for a touch of luxury.

COST OF RENTING A CAR

The average daily cost of renting a car in Barcelona, including insurance, is approximately €36. Prices may vary by month, with summer months typically being pricier due to increased demand.

BOOKING A RENTAL CAR

When booking through car rental platforms, transparency is key. Be cautious of hidden costs that some companies might introduce during the booking process. Carefully select your vehicle, considering size and features, and understand the terms and conditions.

COLLECTING AND RETURNING THE CAR

Ensure you have all necessary documentation for collection, including your driving license, passport, and any required permits. Inspect the car for damage before leaving and take photos if necessary. Similarly, return the car in good condition and go through the check-out process with the rental company.

DRIVING TIPS IN BARCELONA

- Traffic gives priority to oncoming traffic from the right.
- Drive on the right side of the road.
- Use turn signals consistently.
- Seatbelts are mandatory.
- Be cautious with mobile phone use while driving.
- Observe speed limits and parking regulations.

Renting a car in Barcelona can greatly enhance your travel experience. It offers the freedom to explore beyond the city and make the most of your time. By understanding the requirements, costs, and driving tips, you can ensure a safe and enjoyable journey throughout your Catalonian adventure.

Discover cars (*https://www.discovercars.com/spain/barcelona*) is a reliable platform that scours both international and local car rental companies to present options tailored to your preferences.

CHAPTER 2: EXPLORING BARCELONA

CHAPTER TWO

EXPLORE BARCELONA

Exploring Barcelona can be a fantastic experience, as the city is known for its rich history, stunning architecture, vibrant culture, and beautiful Mediterranean coastline. Whether you're interested in art, history, gastronomy, or simply soaking up the lively atmosphere, Barcelona has something to offer you. This Chapter will help you make the most of your visit to Barcelona.

THE 10 DISTRICTS OF BARCELONA

Ciutat Vella (Old Town): The historical heart of Barcelona, Ciutat Vella boasts iconic landmarks such as the Gothic Quarter, the Ramblas, and the Picasso Museum. Its narrow streets and hidden passages are perfect for exploration.

Eixample: Known for its broad avenues and elegant Modernist architecture, Eixample is home to Antoni Gaudí's masterpieces like the Sagrada Familia, Casa Milà, and Casa Batlló.

Sants-Montjuïc: Featuring the picturesque Montjuïc hill with panoramic city views, this district hosts the Olympic Stadium, Palau Sant Jordi, and the Joan Miró Foundation.

Les Corts: A vibrant residential area housing the Camp Nou, FC Barcelona's iconic stadium, Les Corts offers a lively atmosphere.

Sarrià-Sant Gervasi: With upscale boutiques and dining options, this district also showcases attractions like the Tibidabo amusement park and Joan Brossa Gardens.

Gràcia: A bohemian gem with colorful houses, Gràcia is renowned for its eclectic bars, cafes, and artistic vibe.

Horta-Guinardó: This green district boasts lush parks and gardens, and is home to Gaudí's celebrated Park Güell.

Nou Barris: Mixing residential and industrial areas, this diverse district features the Barcelona Zoo and the modernist architecture of Poblenou.

Sant Andreu: A tight-knit community in a working-class setting, Sant Andreu is highlighted by the historic Santa Maria del Taulat church.

Sant Martí: A trendy port district housing the Barceloneta beach and the Olympic Village, Sant Martí offers a modern, coastal atmosphere.

Barcelona's rich tapestry of attractions caters to a variety of interests, ensuring a vibrant experience for every visitor.

TOP 12 MUST-SEE NEIGHBOURHOODS OF BARCELONA

1. GOTHIC QUARTER

The Gothic Quarter in Barcelona, Spain, is the historic core of the city, characterized by its intricate network of medieval streets and buildings, including notable landmarks like the Cathedral of Barcelona, Palau de la Generalitat de Catalunya, and Plaça Sant Jaume. Originally established by the Romans in ancient times, it was further developed by the Visigoths and Moors. During the Middle Ages, it served as Barcelona's cultural and political hub. With its rich history and architecture, the Gothic Quarter has long been a popular attraction for tourists, offering insight into Barcelona's past and culture.

Things To See And Do At The Gothic Quarter

- Marvel at the grandeur of the Cathedral of Barcelona, a significant example of Gothic architecture in Spain that spanned over 600 years in construction
- Stroll through the bustling Plaça Sant Jaume, the primary square of the city.
- Discover the Palau de la Generalitat de Catalunya, housing the government of Catalonia.
- Immerse yourself in history at the Museu d'Història de Barcelona, tracing the city's evolution from its Roman roots to the present.
- Wander through the labyrinthine alleys and narrow streets, veer off the beaten path, and unearth its hidden treasures allowing yourself to get pleasantly lost.
- Indulge in a delectable meal at one of the many charming

restaurants within the quarter.
- Pause for relaxation at the cozy cafes or bars scattered throughout the area.

Uncover the vitality of the Barri Gòtic Market, where the vibrant atmosphere complements the array of fresh produce, seafood, and local delicacies.

2. EL BORN

El Born is a captivating district in Barcelona nestled between the Barri Gòtic and Ribera quarters in the old town. El Born is Characterized by labyrinthine alleys, medieval architecture, and a trendy array of shops and cafes. El Born exudes a distinct allure.

Things To See And Do In El Born

- Embark on a visit to the Picasso Museum, ensconced within a former medieval palace.
- Marvel at the splendor of the Church of Santa Maria del Mar, an exquisite example of Gothic architecture.
- Meander through the enchanting Plaça del Born, a charming square adorned with cafes and restaurants.
- Delve into the vibrant El Born Market, an animated marketplace showcasing fresh produce, seafood, and local delicacies.
- Discover distinctive souvenirs and gifts within the myriad boutiques of El Born.
- Savor a delightful repast or beverage at one of the neighborhood's diverse dining establishments.
- Embark on a tapas crawl through El Born, indulging in delectable fare at the plethora of tapas bars.

- Immerse yourself in contemporary art at MACBA, the Museum of Contemporary Art of Barcelona.
- Savor a leisurely waterfront stroll, basking in panoramic views of the Mediterranean Sea.
- Unwind amidst the parks and gardens that grace the landscape of El Born.

3. EL RAVAL

El Raval, a distinct district in Barcelona, Spain, is known for its multiculturalism, with residents from around the world. Once plagued by crime, it transformed into a hub of art and bohemian culture in the 19th century, followed by becoming an immigrant hub in the 20th century. El Raval maintains its bohemian and cosmopolitan essence, hosting museums, galleries, and a vibrant culinary scene. It's a lively destination offering an authentic Barcelona experience for all visitors.

Things To See And Do In El Raval

- Embark on a journey to the Picasso Museum, the globe's largest institution dedicated to the oeuvre of Pablo Picasso.
- Explore Sant Pau Recinte Modernista, a hospital complex erected during the late 19th and early 20th centuries.
- Immerse yourself in the bustling ambiance of La Boqueria, a renowned public market brimming with a diverse array of fare.
- Venture to El Born Market, a charming locale offering local delicacies and fresh produce.
- Wander the labyrinthine alleyways and byways of El Raval, uncovering its distinctive boutiques, bars, and eateries.

- Revel in El Raval's vibrant nightlife, as numerous bars and clubs keep their doors open well into the night.

4. GRÀCIA

Gràcia, rests atop a hill, offering an artistic and lively ambiance with numerous shops, cafes, and restaurants. It was once an independent village until its incorporation into Barcelona in 1897. With a history of fostering independent spirit and attracting artists and intellectuals, Gràcia remains a vibrant and creative neighborhood, drawing in both residents and visitors.

Things To See And Do In Gracia

- Explore the Plaça del Sol, the central square of Gràcia.
- Roam along Carrer del Verdi, a pedestrian street bordered by shops, cafes, and eateries.
- Visit Casa Milà, a Gaudí masterpiece known for its curving facade and rooftop offering panoramic city views.
- Unwind at Park Güell, another Gaudí creation, adorned with vivid mosaics and whimsical sculptures.
- Dine at the neighborhood's diverse restaurants.
- Taste Catalan cuisine and shop for fresh produce, meats, and cheeses at Mercat de la Llibertat, followed by a café or bar break.
- Attend the Festa Major de Gràcia, an annual August festival showcasing street performers, concerts, and fireworks – a wonderful immersion in local Barcelona culture.

5. LA BARCELONETA

La Barceloneta, situated in Barcelona's Ciutat Vella district, is a coastal neighborhood celebrated for its beaches, seafood eateries, and energetic ambiance.

Things To See And Do In La Barceloneta

- *Beaches:* Embrace the sun and surf at Barceloneta Beach, Sant Sebastià Beach, and Nova Icària Beach, perfect for swimming and relaxation.
- *Promenade:* Meander along the palm-fringed promenade that graces the shoreline – ideal for leisurely walks, people-watching, and picnics.
- *Port Olímpic:* This marina complex, crafted for the 1992 Olympics, offers a hub for yachting, fishing, and aquatic sports.
- *Port Cable Car:* Elevate your perspective on the city and port with the Port Cable Car, offering panoramic vistas.
- *Old Town:* Delve into the captivating old town, a picturesque district featuring narrow lanes and vibrant houses, inviting aimless exploration.
- *Seafood Delights:* Savor the finest seafood in Barcelona at La Barceloneta's renowned seafood establishments, enjoying the freshest catches.
- *Aquarium of Barcelona*: Immerse yourself in the vast Aquarium of Barcelona, showcasing over 11,000 Mediterranean Sea creatures.

6. POBLE SEC

Poble Sec is located between Montjuïc mountain, a hill offering panoramic views and cultural attractions and the Avinguda del Paral·lel. It covers around 70 hectares. It is a lively and diverse neighborhood with a mix of old and new. It is home to a large immigrant population, as well as a vibrant arts and culture scene. The neighborhood is known for its narrow streets, tapas bars, and theaters.

Things To See And Do In Poble Sec

- Visit the Teatre Lliure, a renowned theater company that performs Catalan and international productions.
- Take a walk through the Mercat de les Flors, a flower market that is also home to a theater and dance performances.
- Explore the Plaça del Sortidor, a charming square with a fountain and cafe.
- Sample the tapas at Carrer de Blai, a street known for its tapas bars.
- Enjoy the views from the top of Montjuïc, a hill that offers stunning views of the city.
- Poble Sec is a great option for those looking for a lively and affordable neighborhood with a lot to offer. It is also a good choice for those who are interested in the arts and culture.

7. SANTS-MONTJUÏC

Positioned to the west of Barcelona's city center, Sants-Montjuïc holds the distinction of being the city's largest district. Spanning across 21.35 square kilometers, it is home to approximately 280,000 residents.

Things To See And Do

Montjuïc Hill: Ascend the Montjuïc Hill for stunning panoramic views of Barcelona & visit historical sites like Montjuïc Castle, which narrates the city's past.

Magic Fountain of Montjuïc: Witness the captivating light and water show at the Magic Fountain, a mesmerizing display of music, color, and choreography.

Montjuïc Park: Relax in the expansive Montjuïc Park, perfect for leisurely strolls, picnics, and enjoying nature's tranquility amid the bustling city.

Museu Nacional d'Art de Catalunya (MNAC): Immerse yourself in Catalan art history at the MNAC, featuring an impressive collection of paintings, sculptures, and decorative arts.

Poble Espanyol: Explore the Poble Espanyol, an architectural open-air museum showcasing replicas of Spain's diverse regional villages, along with artisan workshops and boutiques.

Teleférico del Puerto: Ride the cable car to the waterfront for breathtaking views and easy access to the city's maritime offerings.

Arenas de Barcelona: Shop and dine at Arenas de Barcelona, a former bullring transformed into a modern shopping center with a rooftop terrace boasting panoramic city views.

CaixaForum Barcelona: A cultural center known for its innovative exhibitions & events. You can engage with contemporary art & culture.

Botanical Garden of Barcelona: Explore the diverse plant species at the Botanical Garden, offering a serene escape from the urban hustle.

Anella Olímpica: Walk through the Olympic Ring area, a legacy of the 1992 Olympics, featuring iconic venues like the Olympic Stadium and Palau Sant Jordi.

Sant Pau Art Nouveau Site: Admire the stunning modernist architecture of the Sant Pau Art Nouveau Site, a UNESCO World Heritage Site boasting intricate details and captivating gardens.

8. POBLENOU

Poblenou, nestled within Barcelona's Sant Martí district in Spain, has undergone a remarkable transformation. Once a thriving textile industry hub, it has now evolved into a vibrant and trendy enclave.

Things To See And Do

Poblenou Design District: This dynamic nucleus of innovation houses over 1,000 design-centric enterprises. Roam through showrooms, galleries, and workshops, or embark on a guided stroll through this design haven.

Poblenou Beach Exploration: Embrace the sun and sea at Poblenou Beach. A hotspot for swimming, surfing, and relaxation, it also boasts beachside bars and restaurants for delectable bites and refreshing drinks.

Poblenou Cemetery Visit: Engage with history at the picturesque Poblenou Cemetery, where more than 100,000 graves chronicle stories of the past. Notable figures, like architect Antoni Gaudí, find their eternal repose here.

Stroll Along Rambla del Poblenou: Meander through the pedestrian-friendly Rambla del Poblenou, adorned with an array of shops, cafes, and eateries. Immerse yourself in the neighborhood's ambiance and people-watching.

Torre Agbar Visit: Gaze upon the iconic Torre Agbar, a towering skyscraper standing 144 meters tall. Delve into its majesty with a guided tour offering panoramic city views.

Mercado Santa Caterina Shopping: Indulge your senses at Mercado Santa Caterina, a lively market bursting with colors. Discover fresh produce, seafood, and Catalonian culinary delights.

Poblenou beckons as an artistic and trendsetting neighborhood, inviting exploration for those seeking a fusion of creativity and leisure.

9. EIXAMPLE

Eixample is a prominent district in the heart of Barcelona renowned for its expansive boulevards, meticulously structured grid layout, and a plethora of awe-inspiring Modernista architectural wonders.

Things To See And Do In Eixample

- Embark on a journey to the Sagrada Familia, Antoni Gaudí's remarkable unfinished Roman Catholic basilica.
- Behold Casa Milà, also known as La Pedrera, another masterpiece by Gaudí.
- Stroll along Passeig de Gràcia, an elegantly tree-lined avenue graced by a profusion of Modernista edifices.
- Immerse yourself in the legacy of Catalan artist Joan Miró at the Joan Miró Foundation.
- Traverse the vibrant Mercat de la Boqueria, a bustling market offering fresh produce, seafood, and local delicacies.
- Indulge in a culinary delight or a refreshing beverage at Eixample's diverse range of restaurants.
- Enrich your understanding of Eixample's history and architecture through a bike tour.
- Experience the charm of Poble Espanyol, an open-air museum that artfully recreates traditional Spanish villages.
- Explore the myriad boutiques and department stores, engaging in retail therapy.
- Find serenity in the lush parks and gardens that grace Eixample's landscape.

10. SANT ANTONI

Sant Antoni, a burgeoning neighborhood within Barcelona's Eixample district, exudes vibrancy and promise. At its heart stands the 19th-century Sant Antoni Market, a splendid display of Catalan Modernism architecture. Within its walls, a sensory journey awaits, showcasing a diverse array of fresh produce, meats, cheeses, and local delicacies.

On Sundays, the market transforms into a haven for treasure seekers, hosting a bustling book and flea market. Amid its stalls, antique books, vinyl records, vintage attire, and furniture beckon, promising unique discoveries.

Things To See And Do In Sant Antoni

Picasso Museum Visit: Embark on a voyage into history at the Picasso Museum, housed in the former textile factory where the maestro once toiled. Immerse yourself in his early 1900s abode and creative realm.

Exploring the Raval: Delve into the nearby Raval neighborhood, celebrated for its bohemian spirit and captivating street art.

Rambla del Raval Stroll: Traverse the enchanting Rambla del Raval, a pedestrian haven adorned with boutiques, cafes, and bars.

Toast with Vermouth: Partake in local tradition by savoring a vermouth—a Catalan aperitif fusing wine, herbs, and spices—at one of the neighborhood's esteemed vermouth bars.

Culinary Pleasures: Indulge in a culinary expedition within Sant Antoni's diverse restaurants, spanning from Catalan classics to international delights.

TIPS

- To relish a serene market experience, consider an early morning Sant Antoni Market visit.
- The Sunday book and flea market operates from 9 AM to 3 PM.
- Picasso Museum welcomes visitors from 9 AM to 7 PM.
- The Raval neighborhood best unfurls on leisurely walks.
- Public parking options abound in Sant Antoni, albeit at potential cost.

11. SARRIÀ-SANT GERVASI

Sarrià-Sant Gervasi, nestled in Barcelona's northwest, is renowned for its upscale boutiques, eateries, and cafes. The district exudes sophistication and boasts a range of cultural delights including:

CosmoCaixa: A family-favorite science museum with interactive exhibits on space, the human body, and the natural world.

Museu d'Art Modern de Barcelona (MACBA): This modern art haven showcases Catalan and international art from the 20th and 21st centuries.

Fundació Joan Miró: Dedicated to the renowned artist Joan Miró, this museum houses a rich collection of his paintings, sculptures, and drawings.

Parc de la Ciutadella: This expansive park, at the heart of Sarrià-Sant Gervasi, invites relaxation, picnics, and leisurely strolls.

Tibidabo: A hilltop amusement park offering panoramic city views, and home to the majestic Sagrat Cor basilica.

Alongside these highlights, Sarrià-Sant Gervasi is dotted with stylish bars and restaurants, catering to both locals and tourists.

Things To See And Do In Sarrià-Sant Gervasi

Stroll through Sarrià: Explore Sarrià's picturesque streets and traditional Catalan architecture.
Visit Santa Creu de Sarrià Church: Admire the Romanesque beauty of this 11th-century church.
Shop on Passeig de Gràcia: Delight in luxury shopping along this elegant avenue adorned with designer boutiques.
Rooftop Bar Delights: Savor a drink at one of the district's rooftop bars, offering captivating city vistas.

Your journey through Sarrià-Sant Gervasi promises a fusion of cultural indulgence, architectural marvels, and modern elegance.

12. LA RAMBLA

La Rambla, a renowned boulevard in Barcelona stretches 1.2 km (0.75 miles) from Plaça de Catalunya to Port Vell. Lined with shops, eateries, and street performers, it's a vibrant hub for locals and tourists. Divided into distinct sections:

1. Rambla de Canaletes: Fountain of Canaletes; legend says drinking guarantees a return to Barcelona.
2. Rambla dels Estudis: Tied to University of Barcelona; hosts Gran Teatre del Liceu opera house.
3. Rambla de les Flors: Known for flower stalls, bird vendors, and colorful displays.
4. Rambla dels Caputxins: Offers reading materials, kiosks, and more.
5. Rambla de Santa Monica: Artsy, leads to Port Vell, showcases artists and exhibitions.

Below is a list of things to do and see along the La Rambla

iconic boulevard in Barcelona:

1. Leisurely Walk: Enjoy a stroll while observing locals, tourists, performers, and artists.
2. Font de Canaletes: Begin at the iconic fountain, known for its legend of ensuring a return to Barcelona.
3. Gran Teatre del Liceu: Admire the historic opera house, Gran Teatre del Liceu.
4. Flower Stalls: Experience vibrant flower stalls for photos and fragrant moments.

5. Bird Vendors: Witness bird vendors offering feathered companions.
6. Newsstands and Kiosks: Explore stalls with reading materials for a glimpse of daily life.
7. Street Performers: Encounter diverse street performers, remember to tip if entertained.
8. Arts and Culture: Discover cultural exhibitions and art installations.
9. Museu de Cera: Visit the historical Museu de Cera for lifelike wax figures.
10. Miró Mosaic: Pay homage to Joan Miró with a colorful pavement mosaic.
11. Palau de la Virreina: Explore this palace for exhibitions and cultural insight.
12. Dining and Cafés: Relish local cuisine at restaurants, cafés, and tapas bars.
13. Shopping: Browse shops offering souvenirs, gifts, clothing, and more.
14. Boqueria Market: Explore the vibrant food market for fresh produce and culinary delights.

15. Plaça Reial: Visit the nearby square for palm trees, historic architecture, and nightlife.

Take your time to savor these experiences, and be cautious of pickpockets in tourist areas.

TOP 17 MUST-SEE LANDMARKS AND ATTRACTIONS IN BARCELONA

BASILICA OF THE SAGRADA FAMILIA

The Sagrada Familia is an unfinished Roman Catholic basilica in Barcelona, Spain. It's a renowned masterpiece of Catalan Modernism, designed by Antoni Gaudí. Construction started in 1882 and has been ongoing up to the present time.

Address: Carrer de Mallorca, 401, 08013 Barcelona, Spain
Phone: +34 932 01 30 11
Website: https://www.sagradafamilia.org/en
Historical Context: Commissioned by Josep Maria Bocabella, a wealthy Catalan businessman, the project was taken over by Gaudí in 1883. He dedicated his life to the basilica's completion but passed away in 1926, leaving it unfinished.
Visiting Hours: Open to the public from 9:00 AM to 6:00 PM, closed on Mondays. Best times to visit are early mornings or late afternoons to avoid crowds.
Admission: Adults: €26.00; Children (7-12 years): €18.00; Children (0-6 years): Free. (check the website for updates and changes)
Booking: Tickets available online or at the ticket office. It's advisable to make reservations in advance, especially when the high season is in full swing.

THINGS TO SEE AND DO

Admire the Exquisite Facades: Feast your eyes on the intricately adorned exteriors, featuring sculptures and mosaics depicting biblical scenes.
Guided Tours Available: Learn about the basilica's history and construction through guided tours.
Stunning Interior: Discover soaring columns and vibrant stained glass windows within the basilica.

Explore the Crypt: Gaudí's final resting place can be found in the crypt.

Panoramic Roof Terrace: Enjoy breathtaking Barcelona views from the roof terrace.

Partake in Mass: Join any of the daily masses in the active basilica.

PARK GÜELL

Address: Carrer d'Olot, 5, 08024 Barcelona, Spain
Phone: +34 932 16 03 00
Website: https://parkguell.barcelona/en
Description: Park Güell is a public park in Barcelona, Spain, designed by Antoni Gaudí. A prominent work of Catalan Modernism, the park was constructed from 1900 to 1914 and is now a UNESCO World Heritage Site.
Historical Context: Eusebi Güell, a wealthy Catalan industrialist, commissioned the park. Gaudí envisioned it as a utopian community blending with nature, adorned with whimsical sculptures and structures.
Visiting Hours: Open from 8:30 AM until sunset, closed on Mondays. Optimal times to steer clear of crowds are early mornings or late afternoons.
Admission: Adults: €10.00; Children (7-12 years): €7.00; Children (0-6 years): Free.
Booking: Tickets available online or at the ticket office. Advance booking recommended during peak times.

THINGS TO SEE AND DO IN PARK GÜELL

Admire Gaudí's Whimsical Creations: Immerse yourself in the park's playful design featuring Gaudí's organic shapes, mosaics, and sculptures.
Stroll the Serpentine Path: Wander along the iconic serpentine walkway for stunning hillside views.
Discover the Hypostyle Hall: Explore the grand Hypostyle Hall upheld by 86 mosaic-adorned columns.
Capture Barcelona's Vista: Head to the viewpoint for picturesque cityscape photos.
Picnic Amid Nature: Enjoy outdoor relaxation with multiple picnic spots throughout the park.

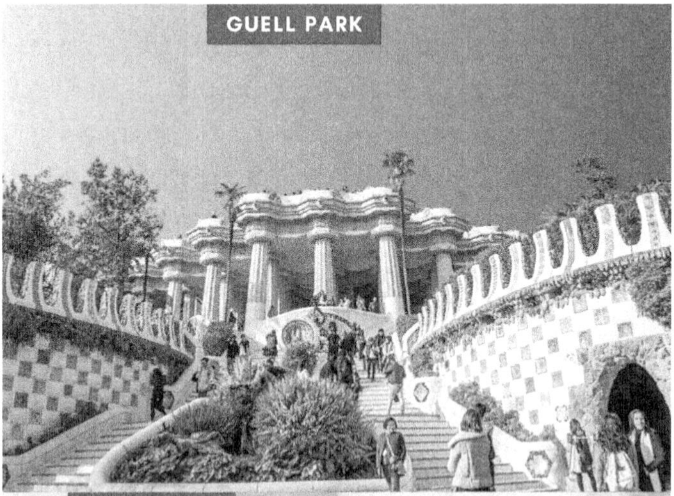
GUELL PARK

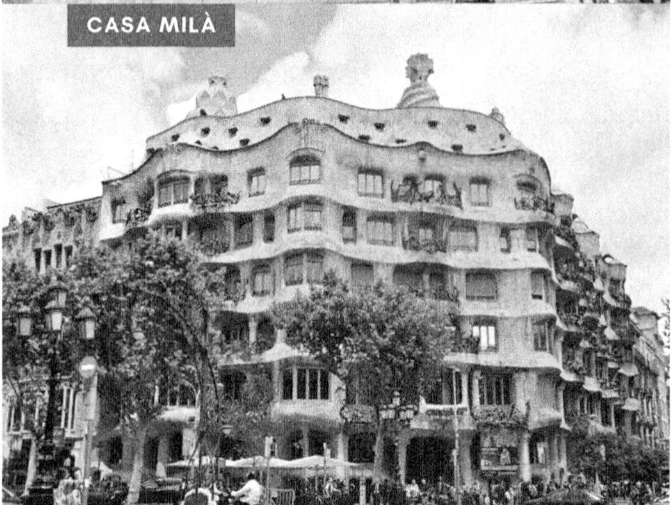
CASA MILÀ

LA PEDRERA - CASA MILÀ

Also called Casa Milà, this modernist masterpiece by architect Antoni Gaudí boasts an undulating stone facade, innovative design, and unique iron balconies. Inside, find exhibitions, a rooftop terrace with panoramic views, and a glimpse into Gaudí's visionary concepts.

Address: Provença, 261-265, 08008 Barcelona, Spain
Phone Number: +34 902 20 21 38
Website: https://www.lapedrera.com
Historical Essence: Erected from 1906 to 1912, La Pedrera emerged as a luxury apartment complex commissioned by Pere Milà and Roser Segimon. Gaudí's groundbreaking style resonates in its organic shapes and functional elements.
Opening Hours: Monday - Sunday, & holidays: 9:00am - 8:30pm, Night tour: 09:00pm - 11:00pm
Admission: Adults: €25, Children aged 7-12: €12.50, Age 6 and below: free
Reservation: To circumvent queues, particularly during peak tourist periods, advance ticket booking is advisable. Tickets can be procured via the official website or on-site.

THINGS TO SEE AND DO

- Admire the artistic exterior composed of undulating trencadis, a mosaic of recycled ceramic tiles.
- Embark on a guided tour to delve into the history and architecture, uncovering Gaudí's designs and the house's symbolism.
- Discover the impressive interior adorned with vibrant tiles and Gaudí-designed furniture.
- Ascend to the rooftop terrace for awe-inspiring Barcelona views and the whimsical mushroom-shaped

chimneys.
- Experience concerts and events held on the rooftop, merging performance with cityscape.

CASA BATLLÓ

Address: Passeig de Gràcia, 92, 08008 Barcelona, Spain
Phone: +34 932 16 03 00
Website: https://www.casabatllo.es/en
Description: Casa Batlló is a private residence in Barcelona, Spain, designed by Antoni Gaudí. A significant work of Catalan Modernism, the house was built between 1904 and 1906 and is a UNESCO World Heritage Site.
Historical Context: Commissioned by Josep Batlló, a wealthy Catalan industrialist, the house showcases Gaudí's innovative style with curvilinear forms and organic shapes.
Visiting Hours: Open from 9:00 AM to 6:30 PM, closed on Mondays. Early mornings or late afternoons are recommended to avoid crowds.
Admission: Adults: €25.00; Children (7-12 years): €18.00;

THINGS TO SEE AND DO IN CASA BATLLÓ

Exquisite Exterior Artistry: Casa Batlló's exterior is an artistic marvel, boasting undulating, colorful features inspired by dragon curves.
Guided Insights: Immerse in history and architecture via guided tours, delving into Gaudí's designs and the house's symbolism.
Elegant Interior Exploration: Step into the impressive interior adorned with Gaudí-designed furniture and vibrant tiled walls.
Rooftop Vistas: Ascend to the rooftop terrace for panoramic Barcelona views and dragon-shaped chimney sightings.

NICHOLAS INGRAM

CASA BATLLÓ

MERCADO DE LA BOQUERIA

Also known as Mercat de Sant Josep de la Boqueria, stands as one of Barcelona's renowned markets on La Rambla. A vibrant hub of fresh produce, seafood, meats, cheeses, spices & culinary treasures, it is enchanting with colorful stalls & a bustling ambiance.

Address: La Rambla, 91, 08001 Barcelona, Spain
Phone Number: +34 933 18 25 84
Website: http://www.boqueria.barcelona/home
Historical Context: Tracing its origins to the 13th century, the market began as a mobile bazaar beyond city walls. Evolving over time, it transitioned into a fixed market and underwent multiple facelifts, cementing its role in Barcelona's culinary and cultural tapestry.
Visiting Hours: Open Monday to Saturday, from 8 AM to 8:30 PM. Mornings offer the liveliest market experience & the freshest produce.
Admission: No entrance fee; payment pertains only to your chosen purchases.
Access: No reservations necessary; entry is open to all.

THINGS TO SEE AND DO

Fresh Fare: Explore stalls brimming with fresh produce, seafood, meat, and a treasure trove of fruits, vegetables, cheeses, and meats.
Taste Local Delights: Indulge in local cuisine at various stalls; don't miss the opportunity to savor tapas, ideal for sharing.
Culinary Classes: Participate in Catalan cooking classes available within the market to learn traditional dishes.
Souvenir Shopping: Browse market stalls for unique

souvenirs, a perfect way to commemorate your visit.

<u>Immersive Experience:</u> Absorb the lively ambiance while wandering; witness captivating sights and activities.

PALAU DE LA MÚSICA CATALANA

Address: Carrer Palau de la Música, 4-6, 08003 Barcelona, Spain.
Phone Number: +34 932 95 72 00
Website: https://www.palaumusica.cat/en
Brief Descriptions: A stunning concert hall known for its intricate architectural design, including intricate mosaics, stained glass, and ornate sculptures. It's a UNESCO World Heritage Site and a symbol of Catalan modernism.
Brief Historical Context: Designed by architect Lluís Domènech i Montaner, the Palau de la Música Catalana was built between 1905 and 1908 as a hub for Catalan music and culture.
Recommended Visiting Times: Guided tours are available throughout the day. Concerts and performances are also held regularly.
Admission Fees: Self-guided tour: adults: €15, Children under 10: Free. Guided tour including a commentary is €19 for adults.
Booking Information: You can book tickets for guided tours and concerts on their official website or at the box office.

WHAT TO DO AND SEE

Attend a concert or performance. The Palau hosts a variety of concerts and performances throughout the year, including classical music, jazz, and opera.
Take a guided tour. The Palau offers guided tours in Catalan, Spanish, English, French, German, Italian, and Portuguese.
Visit the museum. The Palau has a museum that exhibits the history of the building and its collection of art and artifacts.
Have a drink or meal in the cafe. The Palau has a cafe and restaurant that offer stunning views of the Concert Hall.
Take photos. The Palau is a beautiful building and is worth taking

photos of. Just be sure to be respectful of the other visitors and staff.

CAMP NOU - FC BARCELONA'S ICONIC STADIUM

Camp Nou isn't just a stadium; it's a pilgrimage site for global football enthusiasts. The museum showcases the club's history, trophies, and offers a walk through the player's tunnel onto the pitch.

Address: C. d'Arístides Maillol, 12, 08028 Barcelona, Spain

Phone: +34 902 18 99 00

Website: https://www.fcbarcelona.com/en/tickets/camp-nou-experience

History: Inaugurated in 1957, Camp Nou symbolizes Barcelona's football passion. It has evolved through renovations and expansions, accommodating more fans and improved facilities.

Visiting Times: The stadium and museum are generally open throughout the year, with possible variations on match days or events. For accurate details, please consult the official website.

Admission: Adults: €31.50, Children (6-13): €26, Pensioners (65+): €23.50, Children under 6: Free. Alternative experiences available on the website.

Booking: Purchase tickets online or on-site. Buying online, especially during peak times, is recommended.

THINGS TO SEE AND DO

Stadium Tour: Explore the stadium's history and architecture through a guided tour. It includes changing rooms, press areas, and trophy exhibits. You can even step onto the pitch, imagining you're part of FC Barcelona.

Attend a Match: If your timing aligns with a match, don't miss the electric atmosphere at Camp Nou. It's an unforgettable experience.

Visit the Museum: Discover FC Barcelona's journey, from its humble beginnings to its global success, through the museum's exhibits.

Explore the Grounds: Even if football isn't your focus, stroll around Camp Nou's impressive grounds. Feel the history and tradition of FC Barcelona.

CATHEDRAL OF BARCELONA

Address: Pla de la Seu, s/n, 08002 Barcelona, Spain.
Phone Number: +34 933 15 15 54.
Website: http://www.catedralbcn.org
Brief Descriptions: Also known as the Cathedral of the Holy Cross and Saint Eulalia, this Gothic cathedral is a prominent landmark in the Barri Gòtic (Gothic Quarter) of Barcelona.
Brief Historical Context: Construction began in the 13th century and continued over several centuries. The cathedral houses various chapels and features intricate Gothic architecture.
Recommended Visiting Times: The cathedral is generally open to visitors throughout the day. Note that it might be closed during religious services.
Admission Fees: Regular entry at specific times: €7 per person, €5 per person for groups. During free admission times, rooftop and chorus visits are €3 extra per site.
Booking Information: Tickets can be bought directly at the cathedral

WHAT TO DO AND SEE

Visit the exterior. The cathedral's exterior is a stunning example of Catalan Gothic architecture. Take some time to admire the intricate carvings, the spires, and the stained glass windows.
Explore the interior. The inside of the cathedral is equally remarkable as its exterior. Be sure to see the main altar, the choir, and the crypt, which houses the remains of Saint Eulalia, the patron saint of Barcelona.
Take a guided tour. A guided tour can help you learn more about the history and significance of the cathedral.
Enjoy the views from the roof. The cathedral's roof offers stunning views of Barcelona. You can take the stairs or the elevator to the roof.

<u>Attend a mass or concert.</u> The cathedral hosts regular masses and concerts. This is a great way to experience the cathedral's acoustics and beauty.

MOUNT TIBIDABO

Address: Barcelona, Spain.

Brief Descriptions: A mountain overlooking Barcelona with an amusement park and a church at the top.

Brief Historical Context: The Church of the Sacred Heart of Jesus (Temple Expiatori del Sagrat Cor) was completed in the early 20th century and is a prominent landmark.

Recommended Visiting Times: Tmorning, from 10am to 11am, when it is less crowded. Open from 10am to 10pm, but the last entry is at 8pm

Admission Fees: General ticket: Adults: €29.90, Seniors (65+): €26.90, Children (7-16): €19.90, Children under 6: free. Family ticket (2 adults + 2 children): €99.80. Discounted ticket: Students, people with disabilities, and large families: €26.90

Booking Information: You can book your tickets online or at the ticket office at the base of Mount Tibidabo.

WHAT TO DO AND SEE

Visit the Temple Expiatori del Sagrat Cor. The Temple Expiatori del Sagrat Cor is a church that is dedicated to the Sacred Heart of Jesus. It is located on the summit of Mount Tibidabo and offers stunning views of Barcelona.

Go on the Tibidabo Amusement Park. The Tibidabo Amusement Park is a funfair that is located on the slopes of Mount Tibidabo. It has a variety of rides, including roller coasters, carousels, and a Ferris wheel.

Ride a cable car to reach the mountain peak: The Funicular de Vallvidrera is a cable car that takes you up to the summit of Mount Tibidabo. The views from the top are spectacular.

Have a picnic in the park. There is a large park at the summit of Mount Tibidabo where you can have a picnic and enjoy the views.

Go hiking or biking. There are several hiking & biking trails in the area.

Visit the Joan Miró Foundation. The Joan Miró Foundation is an art museum that is dedicated to the work of the Catalan artist Joan Miró. It is located in the Sarrià district, at the foot of Mount Tibidabo.

TIBIDAO AMUSEMENT PARK

MAGIC FOUNTAIN OF MONTJUÏC

MAGIC FOUNTAIN OF MONTJUÏC

Address: Plaça de Carles Buïgas, 1, 08038 Barcelona, Spain.

Brief Descriptions: A large, illuminated fountain located at the base of Montjuïc hill. It's known for its spectacular light and music shows.

Brief Historical Context: The fountain was built for the 1929 Barcelona International Exposition and was designed by Carles Buïgas.

Recommended Visiting Times: The fountain hosts nightly light and music shows. It's a popular attraction, especially in the evening.

Admission Fees: None

WHAT TO DO AND SEE

Watch the water and light show. The Magic Fountain is known for its spectacular water and light show, which is held every half hour from 9:00 to 10:30 pm from Thursday to Saturday from December 22 to March 31. The show features music, water jets, and lights that dance and change color in a synchronized display.

Take a walk around the fountain. The Magic Fountain is located in a beautiful setting at the foot of Montjuïc Mountain. There are plenty of places to sit and relax while you enjoy the show.

Visit the surrounding area. The Magic Fountain is located near many other popular tourist attractions, such as the Palau Nacional, the MNAC, and the Poble Espanyol. You can also take a walk up Montjuïc Mountain for stunning views of the city.

Have a picnic. If you are visiting during the day, you can have a picnic in the park near the fountain. There are plenty of trees and benches to provide shade and seating.

BASILICA OF SANTA MARIA DEL MAR

Address: Plaça de Santa Maria, 1, 08003 Barcelona, Spain.
Phone Number: +34 933 10 23 90.
Website: https://www.santamariadelmarbarcelona.org
Brief Descriptions: This Catalan Gothic basilica is known for its impressive architecture and stunning interior.
Brief Historical Context: The basilica was constructed between the 13th and 15th centuries and is a testament to the maritime and trade history of medieval Barcelona.
Recommended Visiting Times: The basilica is open daily from 10:00 AM to 8:30 PM, with the last entry at 8:00 PM.
Admission Fees: Visit including church, museum, and crypt costs €5 while Guided tour including church, museum, crypt, towers, and terraces costs €13.€5 but entry is free before 1:00 PM and after 5:00 PM.
Booking Information: Advanced booking might not be necessary for general visits.

WHAT TO DO AND SEE

Admire the architecture. The Basilica of Santa Maria del Mar is a beautiful example of Catalan Gothic architecture. The interior is light and airy, with soaring columns and stained glass windows.
Explore the chapels. The Basilica has several chapels, each dedicated to a different saint or religious figure. Be sure to see the Chapel of the Holy Cross, which is home to a beautiful crucifix.
Take a guided tour. A guided tour can help you learn more about the history and significance of the basilica.
Enjoy the views from the roof. The roof of the basilica offers stunning views of the city of Barcelona. You can take the stairs or

the elevator to the roof.

<u>Attend a mass or concert.</u> The basilica hosts regular masses and concerts. This is a great way to experience the basilica's acoustics and beauty.

PICASSO MUSEUM

Address: Carrer Montcada, 15-23, 08003 Barcelona, Spain.
Phone Number: +34 932 56 30 00
Website: https://www.museupicasso.bcn.cat/en
Brief Descriptions: It is dedicated to the works of the renowned Spanish artist Pablo Picasso housed in several medieval palaces.
Historical Context: It is opened in 1963 & features an extensive collection of Picasso's early works, showcasing his artistic evolution.
Ideal Times to Visit: Tuesday to Saturday: 10am to 7pm, Sundays & holidays: 10am to 8pm, Mondays: closed
Admission Fees: Permanent collection: adults: €15, seniors (65+): €12.50, students & children (7-18): €7.50. Permanent collection + temporary exhibition: adults: €19, seniors: €16.50, students & children: €10

WHAT TO DO AND SEE

- Witness Picasso's early journey with a vast collection spanning his childhood to early twenties and experience his distinctive style and artistic experimentation.
- Immerse yourself in Picasso's emotive Blue and Rose periods, characterized by unique color palettes and encounter themes of poverty, sadness, and nostalgia.
- Marvel at Picasso's pioneering Cubist works from the early 20th century and engage with abstract shapes and vibrant colors that define this revolutionary movement.
- Explore Picasso's diverse later works, spanning the 1930s to 1970s. Observe his continued evolution, reflecting experimentation and creative brilliance.
- Opt for guided tours in various languages, exploring the collection and Picasso's life and art.

- Peruse the shop for souvenirs, books, and art inspired by Picasso's legacy.

GÜELL PALACE

Address: Carrer Nou de la Rambla, 3-5, 08001 Barcelona, Spain.
Phone Number: +34 933 17 45 28.
Website: https://www.palauguell.cat/en
Brief Descriptions: Designed by architect Antoni Gaudí for his patron, Eusebi Güell. It showcases Gaudí's innovative architectural style.
Brief Historical Context: Built between 1886 and 1889, the palace reflects Gaudí's unique approach to design and aesthetics.
Recommended Visiting Times: It's advisable to check the museum's website for opening hours and to book tickets in advance.
Admission Fees: Adults (with audioguide): 12 €, 10 - 17 years: 5 €, 0 - 10 years: free entry, Students and 65+: 9 €

WHAT TO DO AND SEE

Admire the architecture. The Güell Palace is a stunning example of Catalan Art Nouveau architecture. The exterior is characterized by its undulating curves and its colorful mosaics. The interior is just as impressive, with its intricate decorations and its unique furniture.
Explore the gardens. The Güell Palace is surrounded by beautiful gardens, which were designed by Gaudí himself. The gardens are full of interesting features, such as the serpentine bench and the dragon fountain.
Take a guided tour. A guided tour can help you learn more about the history and significance of the palace.
Visit the museum. The palace has a museum that exhibits the history of the building and its collection of art and artifacts.

Have a coffee or snack in the cafe. The palace has a cafe that offers stunning views of the gardens.

GUELL PALACE

CIUTADELLA PARK

Address: Passeig de Picasso, 21, 08003 Barcelona, Spain.

Phone Number: +34 010 (Barcelona City Council information line).

Website: *https://www.barcelona.de/en/barcelona-parc-ciutadella.html*, *https://www.barcelonasiempre.com/en/ciutadella-park*

Brief Descriptions: A large urban park featuring green spaces, a lake, sculptures, and historical buildings.

Brief Historical Context: The park was opened in 1877 and was originally designed as a site for the 1888 Barcelona Universal Exposition.

Recommended Visiting Times: The park is open during daylight hours and is a great place to visit on a sunny day.

Admission Fees: Generally, there's no admission fee to enter the park.

WHAT TO DO AND SEE

- *Visit the Cascada Monumental*, a large fountain that is the centerpiece of the park. It was designed by Josep Fontserè and is inspired by the Trevi Fountain in Rome.
- *See the Castle of Three Dragons*, a whimsical building that was designed by Antoni Gaudí. It is now a children's museum.
- *Explore the greenhouses.* The park has several greenhouses that house a variety of plants from around the world.
- *Embark on a boat journey across the lake*: The park has a lake that is a popular spot for boating and paddleboarding.

- *Visit the zoo.* The Barcelona Zoo is located in the park and is home to over 7,000 animals from around the world.
- *Have a picnic.* The park is a great place to have a picnic and enjoy the outdoors.
- *Go for a walk or run.* The park has several walking and running paths that are perfect for getting some exercise.
- *Attend a concert or event.* The park is often used for concerts and other events.

PLAÇA DE CATALUNYA

Address: Plaça de Catalunya, 08002 Barcelona, Spain.

Brief Descriptions: A central square in Barcelona that serves as a hub for transportation, shopping, and cultural events.

Brief Historical Context: The square was designed in the 19th century and has since become a significant meeting point in the city.

Recommended Visiting Times: The square is accessible throughout the day and is often bustling with activity.

Admission Fees: None

Booking Information: No booking is required for general visits.

WHAT TO DO AND SEE

Visit the fountains. The square is home to two large fountains, the Font de Canaletes and the Font del Migdia. The Font de Canaletes is a popular spot for tourists to drink from the water, as it is said to bring good luck.

See the monuments. The square is also home to several monuments, including the Monument to Christopher Columbus and the Font dels Tres Continents. The Monument to Christopher Columbus commemorates the explorer's arrival in the Americas.

Take a walk or sit on a bench. The square is a great place to relax and people-watch. There are plenty of benches where you can sit and enjoy the atmosphere.

Visit the shops and restaurants. The square is surrounded by shops and restaurants, so you can find something to eat or drink to your liking.

Attend a concert or event. The square is often used for concerts and other events. Check the local listings to see what is happening during your visit.

Go shopping. Plaça de Catalunya is a major shopping area, with a variety of stores to choose from.

Take a bus tour. There are several bus tours that depart from Plaça de Catalunya, which can be a great way to see the city.

CASA VICENS GAUDÍ

Address: Carrer de les Carolines, 18-24, 08012 Barcelona, Spain.
Phone Number: +34 932 41 06 78.
Website: https://casavicens.org/en
Brief Descriptions: One of Gaudí's early architectural masterpieces, this house features a blend of different architectural styles.
Brief Historical Context: Built between 1883 and 1888, Casa Vicens showcases Gaudí's creativity and innovation.
Recommended Visiting Times: Check the museum's website for opening hours and book tickets in advance.
Admission Fees: Admission is 16 euros for adults and 12 euros for children and seniors. There is a guided tour available in Catalan, Spanish, English, French, German, Italian, and Portuguese. The tour costs 20 euros for adults and 15 euros for children and seniors.
Booking Information: Advanced booking is recommended.

WHAT TO DO AND SEE

Admire the architecture. Casa Vicens is a beautiful example of Catalan Modernism. The exterior is characterized by its colorful tiles and its Moorish Revival style. The interior is just as impressive, with its intricate decorations and its unique furniture.
Explore the gardens. Casa Vicens has a beautiful garden that was designed by Gaudí himself. The garden is full of interesting features, such as the fountain with the dragon sculptures.
Take a guided tour. A guided tour can help you learn more about the history and significance of the house.
Visit the museum. The house has a museum that exhibits the

history of the building and its collection of art and artifacts.
Have a coffee or snack in the cafe. The house has a cafe that offers stunning views of the garden.

CASA VICENS

14 LESSER-KNOWN PLACES & UNDER-THE-RADAR GEMS IN BARCELONA

Embarking on a journey through Barcelona's enchanting streets unveils a tapestry of hidden gems, waiting to be discovered by the curious traveler. Beyond the well-trodden paths, here lies a collection of captivating sites that often evade mainstream attention. Here's your guide to these Barcelona secrets:

1. HOSPITAL DE SANT PAU

Also known as the Hospital of the Holy Cross and Saint Paul, this is a modernist building complex designed by architect Lluís Domènech i Montaner. It's a UNESCO World Heritage Site and is known for its stunning architecture and intricate details.

Things To See And Do At The Hospital De Sant Pau

- Admire the stunning modernist architecture of the complex, featuring intricate details and vibrant mosaics.
- Take a guided tour to learn about the history and significance of the hospital and its architecture.
- Explore the beautiful gardens surrounding the hospital buildings.

2. BUNKERS DEL CARMEL

These are old anti-aircraft bunkers on a hill in the Carmel neighborhood of Barcelona. They offer panoramic views of the city and have become a popular spot for both locals and tourists.

Things To See And Do At The Bunkers Del Carmel

- Enjoy breathtaking panoramic views of Barcelona from this elevated vantage point.
- Capture stunning photos of the cityscape, especially during sunrise or sunset.
- Bring a picnic and relax while taking in the stunning scenery.

3. MUSEU DE LA XOCOLATA (CHOCOLATE MUSEUM)

As the name suggests, this museum is dedicated to the history of chocolate and its production. It's a delightful place for chocolate enthusiasts, showcasing various chocolate sculptures and exhibits.

Things To See And Do At The Museu De La Xocolata

- Learn about the history of chocolate, its origins, and its journey through different cultures.
- Admire intricate chocolate sculptures and creations on display.
- Participate in chocolate-making workshops and tastings to indulge your sweet tooth.

4. SANTA CATERINA MARKET

This is a vibrant food market in Barcelona, known for its colorful undulating roof designed by Enric Miralles and Benedetta Tagliabue. It's a great place to explore local produce, fresh foods, and other goods.

Things To See And Do At The Santa Caterina Market

- Explore the diverse stalls offering fresh fruits, vegetables, meats, seafood, and other local products.
- Marvel at the colorful undulating roof, which is a work of art in itself.
- Sample traditional Catalan dishes at the market's various food stalls and eateries.

5. PARC DEL LABERINT D'HORTA

This is Barcelona's oldest park, featuring beautifully landscaped gardens and a hedge maze. It provides a tranquil retreat from the urban commotion.

Things To See And Do At The Parc Del Laberint D'horta

- Navigate the beautifully manicured hedge maze for a fun and challenging adventure.
- Stroll through the serene gardens, featuring sculptures, fountains, and ponds.
- Relax in the peaceful atmosphere and enjoy a leisurely picnic.

6. PEDRALBES MONASTERY

A Gothic monastery in the Pedralbes neighborhood, this historic site dates back to the 14th century. It houses the Museu-Monestir de Pedralbes, showcasing religious art and artifacts.

Things To See And Do At The Pedralbes Monastery

- Visit the cloisters and courtyards of the monastery, showcasing Gothic architecture.
- Explore the Museu-Monestir de Pedralbes, which houses

religious art and historical artifacts.
- Learn about the daily life of the nuns who once lived in the monastery.

7. PAVELLONS GÜELL

Designed by Antoni Gaudí, these pavilions were created for the industrialist Eusebi Güell. They display Gaudí's unique architectural style and are now part of the UNESCO World Heritage Site "Works of Antoni Gaudí."

Things To See And Do At The Pavellons Güell

- Admire the unique architectural elements and design features created by Antoni Gaudí.
- Explore the pavilions' interiors and discover the innovative techniques used by Gaudí.
- Gain insight into Gaudí's architectural genius through the exhibits and guided tours.

8. JARDINS DE MOSSEN COSTA I LLOBERA

These gardens are known for their collection of cacti and other succulent plants. They provide a serene environment for plant enthusiasts and those seeking a peaceful stroll.

Things To See And Do At The Jardins De Mossen Costa I Llobera

- Discover a vast collection of cacti and succulent plants from various parts of the world.
- Enjoy a leisurely stroll through the gardens, marveling at

the diverse plant life.
- Take photographs of the unique and exotic plants against the backdrop of Barcelona.

9. MIRADOR DE L'ALCALDE

This is a viewpoint located on Montjuïc Hill, offering panoramic views of the city and the harbor. It's a popular spot to capture breathtaking photographs of Barcelona.

Things To See And Do At The Mirador De L'alcalde

- Capture panoramic views of Barcelona's skyline, including landmarks such as Sagrada Família and Montjuïc Hill.
- Bring a camera to document the stunning vistas, especially during sunrise or sunset.
- Take a relaxing walk around the area and enjoy the natural beauty of Montjuïc Hill.

10. LA PLAÇA – GASTRO MERCAT

La Plaça is a gourmet market located in the heart of Barcelona. It offers a wide range of local and international food products, including fresh produce, meats, cheeses, and more. It's a great place to explore and sample a variety of culinary delights.

Things To See And Do At The La Plaça

- Explore the market's diverse stalls offering fresh produce, meats, seafood, cheeses, and other gourmet products.
- Sample local delicacies and international treats.
- Engage with vendors to learn about Catalan cuisine and

culinary traditions.
- Enjoy a casual meal or snack at the market's food stalls.

11. ROMAN RUINS IN BARCELONA'S GOTHIC QUARTER

Barcelona's Gothic Quarter is home to a rich history, and you can find Roman ruins scattered throughout the area. These ruins are remnants of Barcelona's Roman past and include sections of old walls, streets, and other archaeological sites.

Things To See And Do At The Roman Ruins

- Wander through the narrow streets of the Gothic Quarter and stumble upon ancient Roman ruins.
- Visit the Temple of Augustus, an impressive Roman temple dating back to the 1st century BC.
- Explore Plaça del Rei, which houses archaeological remains of Roman buildings.
- Take a guided tour to learn about the history of the area.

12. TEATRE GREC & GREC GARDEN

The Teatre Grec (Greek Theatre) is an outdoor amphitheater located on Montjuïc hill. It's a popular venue for various cultural events, including theater performances, concerts, and festivals. The surrounding Grec Garden is a beautiful area to explore, offering scenic views of the city.

Things To See And Do At The Teatre Grec & Grec Garden

- Attend a theater performance or concert at the Teatre Grec's open-air amphitheater, especially during the Grec

Festival held in summer.
- Enjoy the panoramic views of the city and the Mediterranean Sea from the theater.
- Take a leisurely stroll through the Grec Garden, filled with lush vegetation and sculptures.

13. FUNDACIÓ ANTONI TÀPIES

The Fundació Antoni Tàpies is a museum dedicated to the work of Catalan artist Antoni Tàpies. It houses a significant collection of his artworks, showcasing his contributions to modern and contemporary art.

Things To See And Do At The Fundació Antoni Tàpies

- Admire a diverse collection of artworks by Antoni Tàpies, including paintings, sculptures, and mixed-media pieces.
- Explore the museum's architecture, designed by modernist architect Lluís Domènech i Montaner.
- Attend temporary exhibitions featuring other contemporary artists.
- Visit the museum shop for art-related souvenirs.

14. ZONA DE BANYS DEL FÒRUM (FÒRUM BATHING AREA)

This area refers to the bathing area located near the Barcelona International Convention Centre (CCIB) and the Fòrum building. It's situated along the coastline and offers access to the sea for swimming and relaxing.

Things To See And Do Zona De Banys Del Fòrum

- Relax on the sandy beaches near the Fòrum area. Take a refreshing swim in the Mediterranean Sea.
- Enjoy beachside cafes and restaurants offering a variety of cuisines.
- Explore the modern architecture of the nearby Fòrum building and the Barcelona International Convention Centre.

TOP 8 MUST-VISIT MUSEUMS IN BARCELONA

MUSEU NACIONAL D'ART DE CATALUNYA (MNAC)

The Museu Nacional d'Art de Catalunya (MNAC) holds a vast collection of Catalan art, from Romanesque to contemporary. The museum showcases over 250,000 artworks, including sculptures, paintings, ceramics, and more. With over 1.2 million yearly visitors, MNAC stands as a prominent European institution, preserving and exhibiting Catalan heritage and artistic achievements.

Location: Palau Nacional, Parc de Montjuic, 08038 Barcelona, Spain

Opening Hours: 10:00 AM - 6:00 PM.

Admission Tickets Price: From around $13.39.

Neighborhood: Sants-Montjuïc

How to Get There: It's a 10-minute walk from Parc de Montjuïc (see pg)

Best Nearby Restaurants: Taps (see pg), La Gastronomica Burgers (see pg), Il Golfo di Napoli (see pg)

Nearby Attractions: Catalan Museum of Archaeology (see page), Mirador Barcelona (Observation Decks & Towers), Palaus d'Alfons XIII i Victoria Eugenia (Architectural Buildings)

THINGS TO DO AND SEE

- Discover the MNAC's extensive art collection, spanning from Romanesque to contemporary works. Highlights include the renowned Romanesque collection with over 100 mural panels, the Gothic collection showcasing art from the 13th to 16th centuries, and the Renaissance, Baroque, Modernista, and Contemporary collections.

- Guided tours in multiple languages offer insight into the collection's history.
- Attend special events like concerts and workshops hosted by the MNAC throughout the year.
- Don't miss the breathtaking views of Barcelona from the museum's terrace.

COSMOCAIXA

CosmoCaixa is a science museum in Barcelona that offers a wide range of interactive exhibits and activities focused on various scientific topics. It features permanent and temporary exhibitions that provide insights into the world of science, from the cosmos and evolution to ecosystems and the human brain.

Location: Isaac Newton, 26, 08022 Barcelona, Spain
Opening Hours: 10:00 AM - 8:00 PM (Open now)
Admission Tickets Price: €6 for adults (16), free for children under 16
Neighborhood: Sant Gervasi-La Bonanova
How to get there: It's an 8-minute walk from the Avinguda Tibidabo metro station. The number 15 bus also stops right in front of the museum.
Best Nearby Restaurants: Mirabe, La Balanza, Asador de Aranda
Nearby Attractions: Monasterio de Santa Maria de Valldonzella, Torre Bellesguard, Rabbies to Montserrat

THINGS TO SEE AND DO

- Discover the Universe Gallery, CosmoCaixa Barcelona's top exhibit by embarking on a cosmic journey from the Big Bang to the present day, learning about stars, planets, galaxies, and more.
- Step into the Rain Forest exhibit. Immerse yourself in a genuine rain forest with towering trees, exotic plants, and wildlife. Get up close to creatures like snakes, monkeys, and butterflies.
- Experience the Amazonian Aquarium, housing 2,000+ aquatic species from the Amazon. Observe their adaptations as they glide through the clear waters.
- Engage with interactive displays. CosmoCaixa

offers numerous hands-on exhibits for dynamic learning. Create tornadoes, explore sound propagation, and design solar systems.

- Hop on the CosmoCaixa Express. Tour the museum effortlessly aboard a miniature train, taking in all exhibits without walking.
- Unwind in the garden—a serene CosmoCaixa oasis. Enjoy diverse flora and take a nature break from scientific exploration.

EROTIC MUSEUM OF BARCELONA
(MUSEU DE L'EROTICA)

This quirky museum in La Rambla is a collection of over 800 artifacts tracing the history and evolution of eroticism and human sexuality.

Location: La Rambla 96, 08002 Barcelona, Spain
Opening Hours: 10:00 AM - 11:00 PM (Open now)
Admission Tickets Price: Tickets from $13.39
Suggested Duration: Less than 1 hour
Neighborhood: El Congrés i els Indians
How to Get There: Nearest metro stations are Liceu (2 min walk) and Jaume I (7 min walk)
Best Nearby Restaurants: **Prado de Flores** - Italian, Seafood, Mediterranean, **Xera Restaurant** - Seafood, Spanish, Healthy, **Bodega Oliva** - Mediterranean, European, Spanish, Wine Bar
Nearby Attractions: Big Fun Museum - Speciality Museums, Mercat del Art de la Placa de Sant Josep Oriol - Flea & Street Markets, Mercat De Sant Antoni - Farmers Markets

THINGS TO SEE AND DO

- *Explore Exhibits:* Discover historical artifacts, art, and multimedia displays depicting human sexuality across cultures and time periods.
- *Admire Art:* See ancient sculptures, paintings, and contemporary artworks that explore themes of desire and sensuality.
- *Learn and Engage:* Engage with interactive displays that provide insights into the history and evolution of sexuality.
- *Cultural Insights:* Gain understanding about

changing societal attitudes toward relationships, gender, and sexuality.
- ***Contemporary Expression:*** Experience modern artistic interpretations of eroticism.
- ***Educational Resources:*** Find information about sexual health, relationships, and consent.
- ***Shop and Relax:*** Browse the gift shop for related items and take a break at the café.

PARC DE MONTJUIC

Parc de Montjuic is a large park in Barcelona, known for its stunning views of the city, historical sites, and green spaces. It offers a variety of attractions, including the Montjuic Castle, the National Museum of Catalonia (MNAC), and the Magic Fountain.

Location: Barcelona, Catalonia, Spain
Website: https://www.castillomontjuic.com
Opening Hours: 10.00 a.m. – 8.00 p.m
Admission Tickets Price: Admission tickets start from $13.39.
Neighborhood: Sants-Montjuïc
How to get there: 7-minute walk from the Parc de Montjuïc metro station.
Best Nearby Restaurants: **La Platilleria** - Mediterranean, European, Spanish cuisine, **Lascar 74** - Seafood, International, Contemporary dishes, **Palo Cortao** - Mediterranean, Spanish, Vegetarian-Friendly
Nearby Attractions: **Montjuic Castle** - A historical castle offering panoramic views of Barcelona, **Jardines De Mossen Cinto Verdaguer** - Beautiful gardens with a variety of plants, **Joan Miro Foundation** - A museum showcasing the works of artist Joan Miro.

THINGS TO SEE AND DO

- Explore the MNAC to discover the world of Catalan art.
- Witness the enchanting Magic Fountain with its synchronized light and music display.
- Stroll through El Poble Espanyol to immerse yourself in traditional Catalan culture.
- Immerse yourself in the artistic realm at the Joan Miró Foundation, housing creations by the renowned Catalan artist.

- Absorb the city's panorama from the heights of Montjuic.
- Indulge in a leisurely walk or bike ride amid the park's green expanse.
- Visit the Olympic Stadium or Palau Sant Jordi for a dose of sports history.
- Savor a delightful picnic amidst the park's picturesque surroundings.

JOAN MIRO FOUNDATION

The Joan Miro Foundation is a dynamic museum that showcases the works of the renowned artist Joan Miró. It also hosts contemporary art exhibitions and is located in a building designed by Josep Lluís Sert.

Location: Parc de Montjuic, s/n, 08038 Barcelona, Spain

Opening Hours: 10:00 AM - 6:00 PM (Closed on certain holidays)

Official Website: https://www.fmirobcn.org https://masmiro.com

Admission Tickets Price: check: https://reserves.fmirobcn.org

Neighborhood: Sants-Montjuïc

How to get there: Accessible via Parc de Montjuïc (4-minute walk) or Poble Sec (9-minute walk) metro stations.

Best Nearby Restaurants: De Paula L'hamburgueseria del Poble Sec, Taps, Xemei

Nearby Attractions: Jardins de Laribal, Jardi de les Escultures, Font Del Passeig De Santa Madrona

Suggested Duration: 1-2 hours

Suggested Itineraries: Combine your visit to the Joan Miro Foundation with a trip to the nearby Museu Nacional d'Art de Catalunya (MNAC) or explore the Parc de Montjuic area for panoramic views of the city.

THINGS TO SEE AND DO

- Immerse in Joan Miró's iconic art – paintings, sculptures, & prints.
- Engage with modern art trends through rotating exhibits.
- Experience Miró's works in a unique, artist-designed building.
- Enjoy stunning Barcelona panoramas from Montjuic Hill.

- Explore sculpture-filled terraces for a serene art-nature fusion.
- Learn through workshops, tours, and programs for all ages.
- Find temporary artworks that complement Miró's collection.
- Shop for unique art-inspired items and books.
- Wander galleries and spaces in a serene, contemplative setting.
- Unwind with refreshments while reflecting on your art journey.

MUSEU D'HISTORIA DE BARCELONA - MUHBA

Explore ancient and medieval Barcelona through extensive underground archaeological excavations beneath Plaça del Rei. Discover the evolution from Barcino to Barcinona, with exhibits showcasing the emergence of the medieval city and a visit to the Palau Reial Major palace.

Location: Placa del Rei, S/N Barri Gotic, 08002 Barcelona, Spain
Website: https://barcelona.cat/museuhistoria/en
Opening Hours: 10:00 AM - 8:00 PM (Check website for any changes)
Admission Tickets Price: €7 (First Sunday of the month - Free entry)
Neighborhood: Barrio Gòtico (Barri Gòtic)
How to get there: Nearest metro stations are Jaume I (1 min walk) and Liceu (6 min walk)
Best Nearby Restaurants: My Way Lounge Restaurant, Cremat 11, Manna Gelats
Nearby Attractions: Capella de Santa Agata (Religious Sites, Churches & Cathedrals), Salo del Tinell (Historic Sites, Architectural Buildings), Placa del Rei (Points of Interest & Landmarks)
Suggested Duration: 1-2 hours

THINGS TO SEE AND DO

- Visit the Royal Palace to explore permanent exhibitions on Roman and medieval Barcelona's history.
- Uncover remnants of Barcino, the Roman city, including a funerary road, necropolis, and ancient walls.
- See the medieval palace, once home to Catalan counts & kings.
- Immerse yourself in Plaça del Rei's ambiance, a medieval

square encircled by significant structures like the Royal Palace, Barcelona Cathedral, and Casa dels Canonges.
- Discover the Frederic Marès Museum, housing over 5,000 Catalan sculptures from the Middle Ages to contemporary times.
- Explore the Born Cultural & Memory Center, which recounts the city's Spanish Civil War history using objects, photos & documents
- Enjoy panoramic views from MUHBA Turó de la Rovira, an observation post in a historic Civil War bunker.
- Participate in diverse workshops and educational activities.

MUSEU MARITIM DE BARCELONA

The Maritime Museum of Barcelona is dedicated to maritime culture and heritage with over 80 years of history. It houses an extensive collection of maritime artifacts and exhibits, including a full-size replica of a 16th-century Spanish galley.

Location: Av. de les Drassanes S/N, 08001 Barcelona, Spain

Website: https://www.mmb.cat

Opening Hours: 10:00 AM - 8:00 PM (Closed now)

Admission Tickets Price: €10 for adults, €5 for concession seniors. Free on Sundays after 3:00 PM.

Neighborhood: El Raval

How to Get There: Nearest metro stations are Drassanes (2-minute walk) and Paral·lel (9-minute walk).

Suggested Duration: 2-3 hours

Best Nearby Restaurants: Bodega Biarritz 1881 Tapas bar, Eat Caribbean Barcelona, Bodega Oliva

Nearby Attractions: Mirador de Colom (Monuments & Statues), El Puerto de Barcelona (Marinas), Barcelona Wax Museum

THINGS TO SEE AND DO

- Explore a vast collection of ships, instruments, and artifacts that tell the story of Barcelona's maritime history.
- Witness ship construction and restoration using traditional techniques in the medieval royal shipyards.
- Learn about maritime technology's evolution and its impact on global exploration through interactive displays.
- See a range of boats and ships, from fishing boats to historic sailing vessels, each with unique stories.
- Step inside the pioneering electric Submarine Peral and discover its role in naval history.

- Temporary Exhibitions: Experience rotating exhibitions that offer fresh insights into maritime themes and history.
- Engage in educational workshops for all ages, uncovering maritime traditions and skills.
- Enjoy Port Vell views as you explore various sections and exhibits.

MUSEO EGIPCI DE BARCELONA

The Egyptian Museum of Barcelona is a private museum that showcases a collection of around 1,200 pieces of Egyptian art, making it one of the best private collections of Egyptian art in Europe.

Location: Calle Valencia, 284, 08007 Barcelona, Spain
Website: https://www.museuegipci.com
Opening Hours: 11:00 AM - 2:00 PM
Admission Tickets Price: Starting from $13.39
Neighborhood: Eixample
How to get there: Passeig de Gràcia (6 min walk), Girona (7 min walk)
Best Nearby Restaurants: **Bella Italia** - Italian, Pizza, Vegetarian Friendly, **Babula Bar 1937** - Mediterranean, European, Spanish, **Lato** - Latin, Cafe, Seafood
Nearby Attractions: Casa Batlló - Architectural Buildings, Casa Amatller - Architectural Buildings, Passeig de Gracia - Scenic Walking Areas
Suggested Duration: Less than 1 hour

THINGS TO SEE AND DO

- Immerse in diverse Egyptian artifacts: statues, sarcophagi, and everyday items showcasing ancient life.
- Discover mummies, tombs, and insights into burial rituals.
- Decode intricate hieroglyphs and their historical role.
- Explore Egyptian gods, mythology, and architecture through models.
- Engage with interactive displays, workshops, and virtual tombs.
- Join expert-led tours, delve into rotating exhibitions.
- Shop for unique Egyptian souvenirs and books.

- Relax and refresh at the café after your exploration.

20 MORE MUSEUMS IN BARCELONA YOU MIGHT CONSIDER VISITING

1. Museu del Modernisme Català: Showcasing the Modernisme movement's artistic and architectural achievements in Catalonia during the late 19th and early 20th centuries.

2. Museu del Disseny de Barcelona: Exploring various design disciplines, including fashion, product design, graphic design, and decorative arts.

3. CaixaForum Barcelona: A cultural center featuring rotating contemporary art exhibitions, as well as cultural and educational activities.

4. Museu Frederic Marès: Housing a collection of sculptures, artifacts, and curiosities collected by sculptor Frederic Marès.

5. Centre de Cultura Contemporània de Barcelona (CCCB): Focusing on contemporary culture and arts through exhibitions, lectures, and performances.

6. Museu de la Xocolata (Chocolate Museum): An interactive museum exploring the history of chocolate and its cultural significance.

7. Museu de la Música de Barcelona: Highlighting the history of musical instruments and showcasing a diverse collection of instruments from different periods.

8. Museu Blau: Also known as the Natural Science Museum of Barcelona, offering insights into the natural world through interactive exhibits and displays.

9. Barcelona Museum of Contemporary Art (MACBA): Focusing on contemporary art, this museum features a diverse collection of works from the latter half of the 20th century to the present day.

10. Museu de la Ciència i de la Tècnica de Catalunya (mNACTEC): Exploring the history of science and technology in Catalonia, showcasing inventions and innovations from various fields.

11. Museu Textil i d'Indumentària: Devoted to textiles and clothing, this museum offers a glimpse into the evolution of fashion and textile production.

12. Museu Arqueològic de Barcelona (MAC): Focused on archaeology, this museum presents artifacts from various historical periods, shedding light on the city's past.

13. Museu de la Moto: A museum dedicated to motorcycles, displaying a collection of vintage and modern bikes, along with related memorabilia.

14. Museu Can Framis: Showcasing contemporary Catalan art, this museum is housed in a former factory building and features a range of artistic styles.

15. Museu de Cera de Barcelona (Wax Museum): Displaying wax figures of historical figures, celebrities, and characters from various periods and cultures.

16. Museu Tèxtil i d'Indumentària Antoni de Montpalau: Offering insights into the history of textiles and clothing, particularly focusing on traditional Catalan attire.

17. Museu Monestir de Pedralbes: Located in a medieval monastery, this museum presents religious art and artifacts, showcasing the history of the site.

18. Museu de la Xarreria: Dedicated to pipes and smoking culture, this unique museum explores the history and craftsmanship of pipes.

19. Museu de Carrosses Fúnebres: Featuring a collection of funeral carriages, this museum provides a glimpse into historical funeral practices.

20. Museu Moto Bassella: Located outside Barcelona, this motorcycle museum houses a wide range of vintage and classic motorcycles.

Depending on your interests, you can choose to explore a combination of these museums to get a comprehensive experience of the city's cultural and historical richness.

VIBRANT FESTIVALS AND EVENTS TO SEE WHILE YOU'RE IN BARCELONA

1. Primavera Sound Barcelona: An internationally acclaimed music festival held in May, featuring diverse artists from various genres.

2. Sónar: A cutting-edge electronic music festival in June that highlights technological innovation.

3. Festa Major de Gràcia: Celebrated in August in the Gracia neighborhood, known for vibrant decorations, street parties, and traditional Catalan dances.

4. La Mercè: Barcelona's main festival in September, offering a week of cultural events, including music, dance, and theater.

5. Poble Espanyol: A living museum with year-round events, including the Festival Grec de Barcelona, a summer arts festival.

6. Festival Cruïlla Barcelona: Held in July, this music festival encompasses rock, pop, electronic, and jazz genres.

7. La Tomatina: An August food fight festival in Buñol, near Valencia, drawing enthusiastic participants from across the world.

8. Circuit Festival: A major July gay pride event in Barcelona, recognized as one of Europe's largest.

9. Formula One Spanish Grand Prix: Held in May, this prestigious Formula One race attracts global attention.

10. Pride Barcelona Parade: Taking place in July, this parade is one of Europe's largest celebrations of LGBTQ+ pride.

11. Festa Major de Sants: Celebrated in August in the Sants neighborhood, known for traditional Catalan dances and culinary delights.

12. Barcelona Beach Festival: A large electronic music festival in July at Parc del Fòrum, among Europe's biggest.

13. Carnaval de Barcelona: A lively February carnival with parades, street parties, and costume contests.

14. National Day of Catalonia: Marked on September 11, commemorating historical events in Barcelona's past.

15. Seville Fair: An April event in Seville featuring music, dance, food, and flamenco.

16. Barcelona Marathon: Held in October, it's one of Europe's largest marathons.

17. Sitges Film Festival: An international October film festival near Barcelona, esteemed in the industry.

18. Barcelona Beer Festival: A September event with a global selection of beers.

19. Castellers de Barcelona: Traditional human tower building performances at various events.

20. Carnival: Celebrated worldwide with parades, costumes, and street festivities.

21. Festival de Guitarra de Barcelona: A September guitar festival featuring global talent.

22. Festa major del Raval: Held in July in the Raval neighborhood, known for its multicultural atmosphere and focus on social justice.

23. Festa de Sant Roc: Celebrated in August in the Poble-sec neighborhood, featuring Catalan dances and delectable food stalls.

THE BEACHES OF BARCELONA

The beaches of Barcelona are renowned for their beauty, accessibility, and vibrant atmosphere. The city is located on the northeastern coast of Spain, along the Mediterranean Sea, and boasts several popular beaches that attract both locals and tourists. Here are some of the most well-known beaches in Barcelona:

1. Barceloneta Beach: Perhaps the most famous beach in Barcelona, Barceloneta Beach is located near the Barceloneta neighborhood. It's characterized by its golden sands and lively atmosphere. The beach is a hub of activity, with beachgoers enjoying sunbathing, swimming, beach sports, and various water activities. The beachfront is also lined with restaurants, bars, and shops.

2. Bogatell Beach: Located just to the northeast of Barceloneta Beach, Bogatell Beach offers a slightly quieter and more relaxed atmosphere. It's known for its clean sands, palm trees, and clear waters. The beach is popular among families and those seeking a more peaceful beach experience.

3. Mar Bella Beach: Mar Bella Beach is situated to the east of Barceloneta Beach and is known for its youthful and energetic vibe. It's a popular spot among the younger crowd and features a designated nudist area. The beach is well-equipped with facilities like sports courts and beach bars.

4. Nova Icaria Beach: Located near the Port Olímpic area, Nova Icaria Beach is a great option for those looking for a more upscale and tranquil beach experience. It's known for its clean and well-maintained environment, making it a family-friendly destination. The beach is also close to various restaurants and the Port Olímpic marina.

5. Ocata Beach: While not directly in Barcelona, Ocata Beach is located in the nearby town of El Masnou, accessible by train. It's a more peaceful and less crowded option for those who prefer to escape the urban hustle and bustle. The beach features soft sands and calm waters, making it suitable for swimming and relaxation.

6. Llevant Beach: This beach is situated in the Poblenou district and is known for its accessibility and family-friendly atmosphere. It features a well-designed promenade with parks, playgrounds, and various amenities. Llevant Beach is a good choice for those who want a more laid-back beach experience away from the city center.

These are just a few of the many beaches you can explore in and around Barcelona. Each beach has its own unique character and attractions, offering a diverse range of experiences for visitors and locals alike. Keep in mind that the popularity of these beaches can vary throughout the year, so it's a good idea to check local information before planning your visit.

BARCELONETA BEACH

BOGATELL BEACH

NOVA ICÀRIA BEACH

CHAPTER 3: BARCELONA DINING AND CULINARY DELIGHTS

Catalunya's esteemed cuisine, influenced by Greek, Roman, and Arab traditions, was celebrated even in the Middle Ages. Despite subsequent shifts, such as the 1714 loss of autonomy and the Franco dictatorship's cultural repression, Catalan food remained constant and adapted to changing times.

Catalunya's journey towards cultural reemergence led to renewed appreciation for its cuisine, though modern challenges include the haste of life and tourist-driven commercialization.

Extending beyond traditional Catalan fare, Barcelona's multicultural heritage is tastefully reflected in its dynamic food scene. Japanese ramen, Peruvian ceviche, and Italian pizza effortlessly find their place alongside local offerings.

Barcelona surely promises a palate-pleasing adventure for every discerning diner whether you crave an authentic taste of Catalonia or seek a culinary exploration.

16 CATALAN DELICACIES TO SAMPLE IN BARCELONA

In the heart of Barcelona, the 16 traditional dishes discussed below offer an authentic taste of Catalan culture, transcending the superficial tourist experience.

1. Pa amb tomàquet: This is a simple dish where country bread is rubbed with ripe tomatoes and drizzled with olive oil. It's a staple in Catalan cuisine and often served as an appetizer or alongside other dishes.

2. Escalivada: Escalivada is a dish made from roasted red peppers, eggplant, and onions. The roasted vegetables are typically sliced and seasoned with olive oil and sometimes garlic. It's often served as a tapa or a side dish.

3. Esqueixada de bacallà: This is a refreshing salad made from shredded salt cod, tomatoes, onions, peppers, and olives. It's dressed with olive oil and vinegar and is a common dish during the warm months.

4. Escudella i carn d'olla: This is a traditional two-course Catalan soup. The first course, "escudella," is a broth with vegetables and often includes pasta or rice. The second course, "carn d'olla," involves serving the cooked meat and vegetables separately with sauce or allioli.

5. Espinacs amb panses i pinyons: This dish consists of sautéed spinach with raisins and pine nuts. The sweet and nutty combination complements the earthy flavor of the spinach.

6. Calçots amb romesco: Calçots are a type of spring onion, similar to a scallion or leek. They are typically grilled and served with romesco sauce, a flavorful blend of roasted red peppers, almonds, garlic, and olive oil.

7. Arròs caldós amb llamàntol: This dish features soupy rice cooked with lobster. The rice absorbs the flavors of the lobster and other ingredients, creating a rich and hearty dish.

8. Arròs negre amb allioli: Also known as "black rice," this dish is made by cooking rice with squid ink, giving it its distinctive dark color. It's often served with allioli, a Catalan garlic and olive oil sauce.

9. Canelons de carn: These are cannelloni pasta tubes stuffed with a meat filling, usually a mixture of ground meat and bechamel sauce. They are baked with cheese on top.

10. Suquet de pescadors: This fisherman's stew is made with monkfish and potatoes. The stew is flavored with a variety of ingredients like garlic, onions, tomatoes, and sometimes almonds.

11. Bacallà a la llauna: This dish involves baking salt cod "on the tin," meaning it's cooked on a baking sheet or tin. It's often seasoned with garlic, parsley, and olive oil.

12. Mongetes amb botifarra: White beans are cooked and served with grilled pork sausages known as "botifarra." This dish is a hearty and flavorful combination.

13. Mandonguilles amb sípia i pèsols: This dish features meatballs cooked with cuttlefish and peas, creating a mix of textures and flavors.

14. Cargols a la llauna: Grilled snails cooked "on the tin." They are often seasoned with a mixture of garlic, parsley, and olive oil.

15. Mel i mató: A simple dessert consisting of fresh cheese (mató) served with honey. The contrast of creamy cheese and sweet honey is delightful.

16. Crema catalana: Similar to crème brûlée, this dessert is a custard with a caramelized sugar top. It's flavored with cinnamon and lemon zest.

These dishes reflect the rich culinary heritage of Catalonia and its emphasis on using local ingredients and traditional cooking methods.

10 BUDGET-FRIENDLY RESTAURANTS AND CAFES

1. LA COVA FUMADA

Established in 1944, La Cova Fumada is a family-operated restaurant that serves classic tapas within a converted wine cellar. It is situated in the Gothic Quarter and renowned for its Catalan cuisine, particularly its delectable grilled meats and fish. The starting price for main dishes is approximately €15.

Address: Carrer del Baluard, 56, 08003 Barcelona, Spain
Phone Number: +34 932 21 40 61
Website: https://www.lacovafumada.com
Service Offerings: Dine-in · Takeaway · No delivery

2. EL XAMPANYET

Found in the heart of the Gothic Quarter, El Xampanyet is a cozy bar offering traditional tapas, cava & wine in casual surroundings with a buzzing vibe. Since 1914, El Xampanyet has been a cherished local gem, delighting patrons with tapas and pintxos. Its main dishes begin at around €12.

Address: Carrer de Montcada, 22, 08003 Barcelona, Spain
Phone Number: +34 933 19 70 03
Website: None (at the time of putting this together)
Service options: Dine-in · No takeaway · No delivery

3. BAR DEL PLA

Nestled in the Raval district, Bar del Pla is a classic and relaxed restaurant & wine bar highlighting no-frills tapas in a homey environment. where you can savor authentic local dishes like "pa amb tomàquet" (tomato-topped bread) and "escalivada" (roasted vegetables). Main dishes kick off at roughly €10.

Address: Carrer de Montcada, 2, 08003 Barcelona, Spain
Phone Number: +34 932 68 30 03
Website: http://www.bardelpla.cat
Service options: in-restaurant dining, takeout, and unfortunately, no delivery is available.

4. LLURITU 2

Located in the Gracia district of Barcelona, Lluritu 2 is a laid-back restaurant spotlighting seafood dishes in a contemporary venue with marble accents. It is celebrated for its extensive array of tapas and friendly service. Prices for tapas start at around €2.50.

Address 1: Carrer de la Virtut, 11, 08012 Barcelona, Spain
Phone Number: +34 932 70 37 52
Address 2: Carrer Torrent de les Flors 71, 08024 - Barcelona
Phone Number: +34 938 553 866
Website: http://www.lluritu.com
Service options: **Dine-in**

5. BO DE B

Offering quick and budget-friendly options, **Bo de B** is a popular counter-service cafe for bocadillo baguette sandwiches, hearty salads & other casual bites with multiple locations across the city, including the Gothic Quarter (Carrer de la Mercè, 35) and the Raval district (Carrer de Joaquin Costa, 38). Sandwiches commence at about €3.50.

Address: C/Merce, Carrer de la Mercè, 35, bajos, 08002 Barcelona, Spain

Phone Number: +34 936 67 49 45
Website: https://web.facebook.com/BodeBCN

Service options: Dine-in · Takeaway · No delivery

6. LA ESQUINA

La Esquina, situated at the junction of Carrer de la Diputació and Passeig de Gràcia in Barcelona's Eixample district, is a tapas haven known for its inventive and diverse offerings. With a bustling outdoor terrace, it's a prime spot for observing passersby. Main dishes begin at around $5.

Address: Calle Bergara, 2 En la esquina de Balmes/Bergara, 08002 Barcelona Spain
Phone Number: +34 937 68 72 42
Website: https://laesquinabarcelona.com/en
Cuisines: Cafe, European, International
Special diets: Vegetarian Friendly, Vegan Options, Gluten Free Options

7. LA PEPITA

La Pepita is an arty, modern space with a small patio burger haven offering mouthwatering Catalan seafood & creative desserts, plus sangria jugs choices starting at approximately €9.

Address: C/ de Còrsega, 343, 08037 Barcelona, Spain
Phone: +34 932 38 48 93
Website: https://www.lapepitabcn.com
Service options: Dine-in · Takeaway · No delivery

8. BRUNCH & CAKE

Indulge in a delightful brunch or sweet treats at **Brunch & Cake**, which offers Breakfast burritos, açai bowls & avo toast, plus baked treats, in a bright space with outdoor seats.

Address 1: C. d'Enric Granados, 19, 08007 Barcelona, Spain
Phone: +34 931 38 35 72
Address 2: C/ del Rosselló, 189, 08036 Barcelona, Spain
Phone Number: +34 932 37 87 65
Address: Pg. de Joan de Borbó, 5, 08003 Barcelona, Spain
Phone: +34 931 40 96 43
Website: https://www.instagram.com/brunchandcake.esp
Service options: Dine-in · Takeaway · Delivery
Special Diets: Vegetarian Friendly, Vegan Options, Gluten Free Options
Meals: Breakfast, Lunch, Brunch, Late Night
Price Range: $4 - $16

9. LA LOLA

La Lola is a vibrant and full of flavor contemporary eatery celebrated for its lively ambiance and delectable tapas. It offers traditional fare like paella, tapas & grilled meats pair with sangria.

Address: Gran Via de les Corts Catalanes, 373, 385, 08015 Barcelona, Spain
Phone: +34 934 25 57 14
Website: laloladelasarenas.com
Service options: Dine-in · Kerbside pickup · No-contact delivery

10. CAN PAIXANO

Can Paixano is a busy traditional bar serving tapas & sandwiches washed down with sparkling wine. Can Paixano is your go-to for traditional Spanish delights. You can enjoy churros with chocolate from around €3.50.

Located in: **Factory Gardens Barcelona**
Address: **Carrer de la Reina Cristina, 7, 08003 Barcelona, Spain**
Phone: **+34 933 10 08 39**
Website: https://www.canpaixano.com
Service options: **Dine-in · Takeaway · No delivery**

7 MID-RANGE RESTAURANTS IN BARCELONA

1. LA GASTRONOMICA BURGERS

La Gastronomica Burgers is a highly rated restaurant in Barcelona, known for its delicious burgers and friendly atmosphere. It offers a variety of burger options, including vegetarian and vegan choices. The staff is attentive and knowledgeable, creating a welcoming experience for visitors.

Address: Carrer Vilamari 9-15, 08015 Barcelona, Spain
Location District: Eixample
Phone: +34 934 24 90 28
Website: https://lagastronomicabcn.com
Service options: Outdoor Seating, Seating, Serves Alcohol, Full Bar, Free Wifi, Accepts Credit Cards, Dog Friendly, Gift Cards Available
Menu: Offers burgers, including vegetarian and vegan options
Price Range: $13 - $16 (USD)

2. VRUTAL

Vrutal is a 100% vegan burger and cocktail bar that offers a variety of vegan burgers and other dishes, along with cocktails. The restaurant is known for its friendly service, innovative vegan options, and a relaxed atmosphere. They have received excellent reviews for their food quality and taste and have received the Travelers' Choice award in 2022. The menu includes options like vegan burgers, cauliflower wings, and various sides.

Address: Rambla del Poblenou No 16 Bajos 4, 08005 Barcelona, Spain

Location District: Poblenou
Phone: +34 934 91 48 06
Website: https://www.vrutal.es/en
Service options: Takeout, Reservations, Outdoor Seating, Seating, Serves Alcohol, Accepts Credit Cards, Table Service, Dog Friendly
Price Range: $9 - $24

3. BELLEBUON

BelleBuon is an Italian restaurant that offers a variety of Italian cuisines, including Neapolitan, Campania, Sicilian, and Southern-Italian dishes. The restaurant is known for its fresh pasta and authentic Italian flavors. The restaurant provides a warm and friendly atmosphere, and customers have praised both the food and the service. The menu includes a range of options for lunch and dinner, and the restaurant offers takeout, outdoor seating, and accepts reservations. The staff is known for being accommodating and attentive, making it a popular choice for Italian food enthusiasts in Barcelona.

Address: Travessera de Gracia, 441, 08025 Barcelona, Spain
Location District: El Baix Guinardo
Phone: +34 935 14 19 71
Website: http://www.bellebuon.com
Service Options: Takeout, Outdoor Seating, Seating, Highchairs Available, Serves Alcohol, Full Bar, Wine and Beer, Free Wifi, Reservations, Accepts Credit Cards, Table Service
Price Range: $11 - $27

4. BLU BAR

Blu Bar offers a variety of vegan dishes including tapas, pizzas, burgers, and desserts. The restaurant is known for its friendly staff, cozy atmosphere, and delicious vegan comfort food. Customers praise the watermelon sangria, vegan pizzas, and other menu items. The restaurant has received excellent reviews for its service, ambiance, and quality of food.

Address: Rambla de Poblenou, 11 Corner with Taulat, 08005 Barcelona, Spain
Location District: Poblenou
Phone: +34 932 21 09 71
Website: https://www.blubar.es/en
Service options: Dine-in, Takeout, Delivery
Cuisines: Bar, Mediterranean, Spanish, Healthy, International, Street Food
Special Diets: Vegetarian Friendly, Vegan Options, Gluten Free Options
Price Range: $3 - $22

5. ZENITH BRUNCH & COCKTAILS

Zenith Brunch & Cocktails is a popular restaurant in Barcelona that offers a variety of delicious and healthy brunch options. The restaurant has a cozy interior and a great vibe. They serve a range of dishes including bagels, tacos, pancakes, and more. The staff, including Felipe, is known for being friendly and attentive, making the dining experience enjoyable. The menu includes gluten-free options and non-alcoholic beverages like daily juices and mocktails. It's a recommended spot for those looking for a satisfying brunch experience in Barcelona.

Address: Gran Via de les Corts Catalanes, 633, 08010 Barcelona, Spain
Location District: Eixample

Phone: +34 931 96 70 59
Website: https://www.zenithcaffe.es/en
Service options: Breakfast, Lunch, Dinner, Brunch
Menu: Cafe, International, Healthy
Price Range: $8 - $15

6. TAPS

Taps offers a delightful Mediterranean culinary experience in a cozy setting near the Magic Fountain in Montjuic (see pg). With a range of options including tapas and local cuisine, the restaurant is praised for its exceptional food, friendly staff, and charming atmosphere. It's a well-loved destination for both tourists and residents.

Address: C/ Mare de Deu del Remei, 53, 08004 Barcelona, Spain
Location District: Sants-Montjuic
Phone: +34 936 25 80 66
Website: https://tapsbarcelona.com
Service Options: Seating, Parking Available, Serves Alcohol, Full Bar, Wine and Beer, Accepts Mastercard, Accepts Visa, Free Wifi, Reservations, Street Parking, Accepts Credit Cards, Table Service
Price Range: $13 - $24
Culinary Experiences: Mediterranean, European, Spanish, Catalan
Notable Dishes and Drinks: Padron Peppers, goat cheese with honey, slow-cooked pork tacos, sangria, patatas bravas, Spanish omelet

7. IL GOLFO DI NAPOLI

Italian restaurant offering simple and authentic Italian cuisine, including pizza and pasta.

Address: Lleida 38, 08004 Barcelona, Spain

Location District: Sants-Montjuic
Restaurant Type: Mid-range
Phone: +34 934 23 45 43
Website: https://www.ilgolfodinapoli.com/en/
Service Options: Takeout, Delivery
Price Range: $23 - $31
Culinary Experiences: Italian, Pizza, Mediterranean, European
Notable Dishes and Drinks: Seafood lasagna, pizza with ashes and zucchini flowers, pistachio tiramisu, chocolate cakes

5 FINE DINING RESTAURANTS IN BARCELONA

1. XERA RESTAURANT

Xera Restaurant is a highly-rated dining establishment with ambiance characterized as family-friendly, with options for private dining and a full bar. Reservations are recommended due to its popularity.

Address: Calle De Les Sitges 10, Barcelona, 08001, Spain
Location District: Gothic Quarter (Barri Gòtic)
Phone: +34 685 14 76 29
Website: https://raobcn.com/es/inicio
Service options: Reservations, Private Dining, Wine and Beer, Digital Payments, Free Wifi, Family style, Non-smoking restaurants
Menu: The menu includes dishes such as "Jamón Ibérico," "Bravas Xera," "Burrata Pugliese," "Tortilla de Patata," "Carrillera Ibérica," "Ceviche Xera," "Tartar de Atún Rojo," "Ensalada de Verduras," "Tagliata de Magret de Pato," "Pulpo a la Brasa," and more.
Price Range: $20 - $80
Culinary Experiences: Spanish, Catalan, Seafood, Healthy
Notable Dishes and Drinks: Jamón Ibérico, Bravas Xera, Burrata Pugliese, Ceviche Xera, Pulpo a la Brasa, and other tapas and seafood dishes.

2. CON GRACIA

Con Gracia is known for its exceptional service, personalized experience, and carefully crafted dishes. The restaurant has received high ratings and positive reviews for its food quality, atmosphere, and attentive staff. It's suitable for special occasions and those looking for an elevated dining experience in

Barcelona.

Address: Martinez de la Rosa 8, 08012 Barcelona, Spain
Location District: Gracia
Phone: +34 932 38 02 01
Website: https://congraciarestaurant.com
Service options: Fine Dining, Tasting Menu
Menu: "Menú experiencia" - A tasting menu featuring Mediterranean, Spanish, Healthy, Catalan, Fusion cuisines and wine pairings
Price Range: $75 - $108
Culinary Experiences: Mediterranean, Spanish, Healthy, Catalan, Fusion
Notable Dishes and Drinks: Tasting menu with various courses,

3. LAB RESTAURANT

LAB Restaurant offers an innovative and creative dining experience with an experimental tasting menu. The restaurant is known for its imaginative presentation and unique combinations of flavors. Each course is carefully crafted and visually appealing. The intimate setting and personalized service contribute to a memorable dining experience. The tasting menu consists of 19 courses that showcase the chef's creativity and culinary expertise.

Address: Carrer de Rossend Arús 12 Local 2, 08014 Barcelona, Spain
Location District: Sants
Phone: +34 699 26 49 67
Website: https://www.labrestaurant.es/en
Service options: Fine Dining, Tasting Menu
Menu: Experimental and imaginative tasting menu
Price Range: $70

Culinary Experiences: Mediterranean, European, Spanish
Notable Dishes & Drinks: Innovative & creative dishes, 19-course menu

4. SATO I TANAKA

Sato I Tanaka is known for its authentic and high-quality Japanese cuisine. The restaurant offers a tasting menu featuring an assortment of meticulously prepared sushi dishes. With a focus on fresh seafood and attention to detail, Sato I Tanaka provides an intimate dining experience with a menu that showcases the artistry of Japanese cuisine.

Address: Bruc, 79, 08009 Barcelona, Spain
Location District: Eixample, Barcelona
Phone: +34 938 09 92 74
Website: http://satotanaka.com
Service options: Fine Dining
Price Range: $24 - $108
Culinary Experiences: Japanese, Sushi, Asian, Healthy
Notable Dishes and Drinks: Exquisite quality fresh seafood nigiris & makis

5. SANTA RITA EXPERIENCE

Santa Rita Experience is a highly acclaimed restaurant known for its exceptional food and intimate dining experience. With a focus on flavor, creativity, and freshness, the restaurant offers a tasting menu featuring unique Mediterranean and fusion dishes. The setting allows diners to observe the kitchen and interact with the chef, adding to the overall experience.

Address: Carrer de Veneçuela 16, 08019 Barcelona, Spain
Location District: Provencals del Poblenou, Barcelona

Phone: +34 676 27 28 20

Website: https://santaritaexperience.com

Service options: Fine Dining

Price Range: $65 - $98

Culinary Experiences: Mediterranean, Spanish, European, Fusion

Notable Dishes & Drinks: Intricate, delicate, and flavorful 7-course selections with wine pairings

STREET FOOD AND MARKETS IN BARCELONA

Mercat de La Boqueria: Situated along Las Ramblas, this renowned market is a must-visit for food enthusiasts. With a vibrant array of stalls, it offers fresh produce, seafood, meats, cheeses, and prepared dishes, including tapas, paella, and churros.

Mercat de Santa Caterina: Found in the Eixample district, this market is celebrated for its colorful modernist architecture. It boasts a diverse range of stalls offering fresh produce, seafood, meats, cheeses, and prepared foods.

Palo Alto Market: Taking place in the Poblenou district every weekend, this street food market showcases local vendors' culinary delights, complemented by live music and entertainment.

Eat Street Market: Nestled in the Gràcia district, this street food market offers an assortment of global cuisines from its various stalls.

Van Van Market: Located in the Born district, this street food market features local food stalls along with craft beer and cocktails.

DIETARY PREFERENCES AND RESTRICTIONS

Barcelona stands out as a highly accommodating city for individuals with diverse dietary preferences and restrictions. Consider the following guidelines for dining in Barcelona:

Vegetarian and Vegan Options Abound: Numerous dining establishments feature exclusive vegetarian or vegan menus. Even those without dedicated menus frequently offer vegetarian choices.
Increasing Availability of Gluten-Free Fare: Barcelona houses a variety of gluten-free restaurants, while many other eateries can readily fulfill gluten-free requests.
Notify Restaurants of Specific Dietary Needs: For individuals with distinct dietary limitations like nut allergies, it's advisable to communicate your requirements when reserving a table. Most restaurants are eager to accommodate such needs.

Below are specific venues in Barcelona that cater to different dietary preferences and restrictions:

VEGETARIAN AND VEGAN RESTAURANTS

Green Spot: A well-known vegetarian restaurant renowned for its diverse range of dishes.
Veggie Garden: Another excellent choice for vegetarian fare.
La Guineu: A vegan restaurant celebrated for its delectable Catalan cuisine.

GLUTEN-FREE RESTAURANTS

Gluten Free Barcelona: A specialized restaurant offering gluten-free culinary delights.

La Donuteria: A must-visit gluten-free donut shop, perfect for those with a sweet tooth.

El Jardí: A gluten-free restaurant providing Catalan cuisine.

CHAPTER 4: ACCOMMODATIONS

When planning your vacation to Barcelona, selecting the right accommodation is essential for a comfortable and enjoyable stay. Barcelona offers a wide range of lodging options to suit various preferences and budgets.

CHOOSING THE RIGHT ACCOMMODATION

1. Location Matters: Consider where you want to be based. Barcelona has diverse neighborhoods, each with its own charm and attractions. Decide whether you prefer a bustling city center, a beachfront area, or a quieter residential district.

2. Budget: Determine your budget range for accommodation. Barcelona provides options that cater to different financial considerations, from luxury hotels to budget-friendly hostels.

3. Travel Companions: Consider who you're traveling with. Families might prefer spacious apartments, while solo travelers might opt for social hostels.

4. Amenities and Services: Decide which amenities are important to you, such as free Wi-Fi, fitness facilities, room service, or a pool.

5. Reviews and Ratings: Research online reviews and ratings to get a sense of previous guests' experiences at various accommodations.

ACCOMMODATION OPTIONS

Diverse lodging that suits all budgets are available in Barcelona

Hostels: Ideal for budget travelers, hostels offer shared dorms, private rooms, and communal spaces. Notables includes Generator Barcelona, Albergue Pere Tarrés Barcelona, and Hostal Europa.

Budget Hotels: Privacy and comfort define budget hotels, with private rooms and en suite facilities. Hotel Astoria, Travelodge Barcelona Poblenou, and Hotel Europark are popular.

Mid-Range Hotels: Balancing price and comfort, these hotels offer en suite rooms with amenities like AC, breakfast, and Wi-Fi. Hotel Soho Barcelona, Seventy Barcelona, and H10 Madison are well-regarded.

Luxury Hotels: Unparalleled comfort awaits with spacious rooms, 24/7 room service, pools, and spas. Consider W Barcelona, Hotel Arts Barcelona, and Mandarin Oriental, Barcelona.

6 BEST BUDGET FRIENDLY LODGING RECOMMENDATION IN BARCELONA

1. TRAVELODGE BARCELONA POBLENOU

Travelodge Barcelona Poblenou is a **budget hotel** located in the Poblenou district of Barcelona. It offers comfortable and spacious rooms with air conditioning and internet access. The hotel features a 24-hour Bar-Cafe, free unlimited Wi-Fi in public areas, meeting rooms, private underground parking, and a terrace bar.

Address: Carrer Llull, 170, 08005 Barcelona, Spain

Facilities and Amenities: Paid private parking on-site, Wi-Fi, Bar/lounge, Baggage storage, Non-smoking hotel, 24-hour front desk, Express check-in/check-out, Air conditioning, Flatscreen TV, Bath/shower, Complimentary toiletries, Family rooms, Non-smoking rooms.

Dining Options: On-site restaurant, Bar-Cafe, Terrace Bar.

Price Range: $108 - $160 based on average rates for a standard Room

Booking Information: official website: https://travelodge.es/travelodge-barcelona-destiny/travelodge-barcelona-poblenou-hotel or various online travel agencies.

Nearby Attractions: El Poblenou, Rambla del Poblenou, Madame George Lounge Bar

Safety and Accessibility: offers reduced mobility rooms & wheelchair access.

2. SAFESTAY BARCELONA PASSEIG DE GRACIA

Safestay Barcelona Passeig De Gracia is a **hostel** located on Passeig de Gràcia in Barcelona, Spain. It offers budget accommodation with various amenities.

Address: Passeig De Gracia 33, 08007 Barcelona, Spain

Facilities and Amenities: The hostel offers free internet, a bar/lounge, game room, hiking, rooftop terrace, baggage storage, 24-hour front desk, laundry service, housekeeping, and more.

Dining Options: There is a rooftop bar and lounge available.

Reviews and Ratings: The hostel has received mixed reviews, with some travelers praising its location and others expressing concerns about cleanliness, safety, and customer service.

Price Range: The average nightly price is around $103.

Booking Information: Reservations can be made through Booking.com.

Nearby Attractions: Nearby attractions include Casa Batlló, Bobby's Free, and Typical Adult Behavior.

3. GENERATOR BARCELONA

Generator Barcelona is a modern and trendy **hostel** located in the Vila de Gràcia neighborhood of Barcelona, Spain. It offers a stylish and vibrant atmosphere with various room types and amenities for travelers.

Address: Carrer De Còrsega, 373, 08037 Barcelona, Spain

Facilities and Amenities: The hostel offers a range of amenities, including free high-speed internet (WiFi), a bar/lounge, bicycle rental, game room, 24-hour security, baggage storage, and a 24-hour check-in. Room features include air conditioning, desk, private balcony, and bath/shower. Different room types are available, including non-smoking rooms and family rooms.

Dining options: The hostel has an on-site restaurant and bar/

lounge where guests can enjoy meals and drinks. There's also a communal TV room, an outdoor patio, and a chill-out lounge/café.

Reviews and Ratings: The hostel has received positive reviews, with an average rating of 4.0 out of 5 based on 2,271 reviews. Guests have praised its location, cleanliness, service, and value.

Price range: The average nightly price ranges from $58 to $116.

Booking information: Bookings can be made through various online platforms like TripAdvisor, or directly through the hostel's website at: *https://staygenerator.com/hostels/barcelona*

Nearby Attractions: Passeig de Gracia, Casa Milà - La Pedrera, Bloody Mary Cocktail Lounge, Despacio Spa at The One

Safety and Accessibility: The hostel offers 24-hour security and has wheelchair accessibility.

4. CASA GRACIA

Casa Gracia is a unique and stylish hostel located in the heart of Barcelona, offering a vibrant atmosphere and comfortable accommodations for travelers.

Address: Passeig de Gracia 116, 08008 Barcelona, Spain

Facilities and Amenities: Paid public parking nearby, Free High-Speed Internet (WiFi), Bar/lounge, Evening entertainment, Airport transportation, 24-hour security, Baggage storage, 24-hour front desk, Air conditioning, Private balcony

Dining Options: Breakfast buffet available with outdoor seating area, on-site bar/lounge.

Price Range: $106 - $187 based on average rates for a standard room

Booking Information: Available deals on Expedia.com

Nearby Attractions: Passeig de Gracia, Casa Milà - La Pedrera,

Scenic Walking Areas, Architectural Buildings, Bars & Clubs, Spas

<u>Safety and Accessibility:</u> Wheelchair access, reduced mobility rooms, and facilities for disabled guests are available.

<u>Additional Information:</u> Positive comments on helpful and friendly staff, cleanliness, location, and facilities.

5. ST CHRISTOPHER'S INN BARCELONA

St Christopher's Inn Barcelona is a <u>hostel</u> located at the top of Barcelona's famous La Rambla. It offers modern facilities, individual charging points, private curtains on every dorm bed and more. The hostel has a 24-hour reception and offers a range of trips and tours.

<u>Address:</u> Calle Bergara 3, 08002 Barcelona, Spain

<u>Facilities & Amenities:</u> Free internet, bar/lounge, bicycle rental, billiards, baggage storage, non-smoking hotel, 24-hour front desk, laundry service, air conditioning in rooms, non-smoking rooms, free walking tours, etc.

<u>Dining Options:</u> Onsite Belushi's bar and restaurant offering discounts on food and drinks. Continental breakfast included.

<u>Reviews & Ratings:</u> The hostel has a rating of 4.0 based on 1,329 reviews. The reviews highlight the cleanliness, service, value, & location.

<u>Price Range:</u> $50 - $277 based on average rates for a standard room

<u>Booking Information:</u> The hostel can be booked through various platforms like Booking.com.

<u>Nearby Attractions</u>: Located near La Whiskeria, 123 Action Barcelona, Typical Adult Behavior, and other attractions.

<u>Safety and Accessibility:</u> The hostel has safety measures in

place, including limited access areas with room cards.

6. SMARTROOM BARCELONA

SmartRoom Barcelona is a budget hospitality accommodation with modern and functional rooms, each with their own private bathroom. The hotel is designed with a clean and minimalist style, offering comfortable and quiet spaces. Essential services are included to provide customers with the best price.

Address: 56 Carrer Olzinelles, 08014 Barcelona, Spain

Facilities and Amenities: Free High-Speed Internet (WiFi), Vending machine, Baggage storage, Concierge, Non-smoking hotel, 24-hour front desk, Air conditioning, Housekeeping, Private balcony, Safe, Flatscreen TV

Dining Options: The hotel offers breakfast, and there are cafes and restaurants nearby.

Price Range: $92 - $110 based on average rates for a standard room. Prices may vary based on the travel dates.

Booking Information: The hotel can be booked through various online travel platforms.

Nearby Attractions: MUTANT X-PERIENCE (Action Room Escape)

Unreal Room Escape Sants, Mercat de Sants, Room Escape Kessler Galimany

Safety and Accessibility: The hotel offers reduced mobility rooms and facilities for disabled guests. It also provides wheelchair access.

5 BEST MID-RANGE LODGING RECOMMENDATION

1. NOBU HOTEL BARCELONA

Nobu Hotel Barcelona is a luxury lifestyle hotel located in the Sants-Montjuïc district of Barcelona. It offers 259 sleek and spacious accommodations, an elegant spa and gym, meeting and event spaces, the world-class Nobu Restaurant, and Kozara – a laidback lobby bar.

Address: Avenida de Roma, 2-4, 08014 Barcelona, Spain

Facilities and Amenities: Paid private parking on-site, Free High-Speed Internet (WiFi), Fitness Center with Gym/Workout Room, Bar/lounge, Business Center with Internet Access, Room features such as blackout curtains, soundproof rooms, air conditioning, coffee/tea maker, etc.

Dining Options: Nobu Restaurant and Kozara lobby bar

Reviews and Ratings: The hotel has received 4.0 out of 5 stars on average from 97 reviews. The location is rated 3.9, cleanliness 4.6, service 4.3, and value 4.2.

Price Range: $200 - $322 based on Average Rates for a Standard Room

Booking Information: Bookings can be made through their website: https://barcelona.nobuhotels.com or booking platforms like Booking.com.

Nearby Attractions: Red Helmet Experience - Barcelona, Estación De Barcelona Sants, Parc de Joan Miró, Parque de la España Industrial

2. THE LEVEL AT MELIA BARCELONA SKY

Situated in Barcelona's Poblenou district, The Level at Melia Barcelona Sky is a luxurious hotel that offers personalized services, modern amenities, and stunning city and sea views.

Address: C/ Lope de Vega, 141-147, 08005 Barcelona, Spain

Facilities and Amenities: Rooftop bar, free high-speed internet (WiFi), pool, fitness center, free breakfast, business center, conference facilities, spa, air conditioning, fireplace, room service, safe, minibar, flatscreen TV, ocean view rooms, non-smoking rooms, suites, family rooms.

Dining Options: On-site restaurant, Level Lounge with snacks and drinks.

Reviews and Ratings: 4.5 out of 5 (Excellent) based on 896 reviews on TripAdvisor. Ranked #161 of 549 hotels in Barcelona.

Price Range: $258 - $365 based on Average Rates for a Standard Room

Booking Information: Reservations can be made on the hotel's website: *https://www.melia.com/en/hotels/spain/barcelona/the-level-at-melia-barcelona-sky* or by calling 009 1 888-575-2385.

Nearby Attractions: Mystery Escape, Madame George Lounge Bar, Top Secret Room Escape, Poblenou neighborhood, Barcelona beaches.

Safety and Accessibility: Elevator accessibility for all guests.

Check-in and Check-out Times: Check-in time is typically in the afternoon, and check-out time is usually in the morning.

Additional Information: The hotel offers a private lounge, special in-room amenities, and superior room categories as part of The Level experience. The property is known for its Platinum level GreenLeaders certification.

3. MELIÁ BARCELONA SARRIÀ

Meliá Barcelona Sarrià is a hotel located in the financial, cultural, and commercial heart of Barcelona. It offers a strategic location for both business and leisure travelers.

Address: Avinguda de Sarrià 50, 08029 Barcelona, Spain

Facilities and Amenities: The hotel offers various amenities, including paid private parking on-site, free high-speed internet (WiFi), a hot tub, a fitness center with a gym/workout room, a bar/lounge, bicycle rental, highchairs available, and taxi service. Room features include blackout curtains, air conditioning, a desk, fireplace, housekeeping, minibar, cable/satellite TV, and walk-in shower.

Dining Options: The hotel has an on-site restaurant where guests can enjoy meals. Breakfast is also available.

Reviews and Ratings: The hotel has received positive reviews, with a rating of 4.0 out of 5 based on 3,177 reviews on TripAdvisor. Guests have praised the staff, service, and location.

Price Range: $176 to $309, depending on the type of room & availability.

Booking Information: Reservations can be made through the hotel's official website: *https://www.melia.com/en/hotels/spain/barcelona/melia-barcelona-sarria* or other booking platforms.

Nearby Attractions: KAHALA Barcelona, Konbe Cocktail Bar, and Byblos.

Safety and Accessibility: The hotel provides various safety features, and it offers easy access to attractions and public transportation.

Pet-Friendly Policy: pets are not allowed.

4. HOTEL OHLA BARCELONA

Hotel Ohla Barcelona is a five-star *boutique hotel* located in the historical center of Barcelona. It offers a fusion of calm serenity and the bustle of downtown Barcelona. The hotel features a rooftop pool and bar, on-site dining options, and luxurious accommodations.

Address: Via Laietana 49, 08003 Barcelona, Spain

Facilities and Amenities: rooftop bar, rooftop pool, fitness center, spa, sauna, massage room, on-site restaurant (Caelis restaurant), tapas restaurant (La Plassohla), boutique bar (Vistro 49), meeting rooms, internet corner, and parking garage.

Dining options: The hotel's dining options include Caelis restaurant (awarded with a Michelin star), La Plassohla (tapas and small plates), and Vistro 49 (a boutique bar specialized in wines and cocktails).

Reviews and Ratings: The hotel has received excellent reviews from travelers, with an average rating of 4.5 out of 5.0 based on 2,487 reviews. Guests have praised the staff, location, cleanliness, service, and value.

Price range: The average nightly price *$307 to $461.*

Booking information: Bookings can be made through various online travel platforms or the hotel's official website: *https://www.ohlabarcelona.com*

Nearby Attractions: Palace of Catalan Music, Maximum Escape 3, Generation Tours, and more.

5. KIMPTON VIVIDORA HOTEL

Kimpton Vividora Hotel is a stylish and modern boutique hotel located in the heart of Barcelona's Gothic Quarter. It offers a prime location for exploring the city and features a rooftop bar with great views, a rooftop pool, and comfortable rooms.

Address: Carrer del Duc 15, 08002 Barcelona, Spain

Website: *https://shorturl.at/fgiVY*
Facilities and Amenities: Rooftop bar with great views, Rooftop pool, Free high-speed internet (WiFi), Fitness center with gym/workout room, Bar/lounge, Bicycle rental, Babysitting services, Blackout curtains, Soundproof rooms, Air conditioning, Housekeeping, Coffee/tea maker, Cable/satellite TV, Walk-in shower, City view and landmark view rooms available, Non-smoking rooms and suites, Family rooms
Dining Options: Rooftop bar and an on-site restaurant.
Reviews and Ratings: The hotel has received excellent reviews, with an average traveler rating of 5.0 out of 5.0 based on 417 reviews. It is ranked #30 out of 549 hotels in Barcelona.
Price Range: $310 - $427 based on average rates for a standard room
Booking Information: Bookings can be made through the hotel's official website or booking platforms like Booking.com.
Nearby Attractions: The hotel is within walking distance of attractions like Barcelona Cathedral, La Rambla, Gothic Quarter, and the Palace of Catalan Music.
Safety and Accessibility: The hotel offers facilities for disabled guests, and it is mentioned to be wheelchair accessible.

6. NH COLLECTION BARCELONA GRAN HOTEL CALDERON

NH Collection Barcelona Gran Hotel Calderon is a modern 4.5-star hotel located in the heart of Barcelona's city center. It offers excellent service, a rooftop bar with panoramic views, and comfortable accommodations.
Address: Rambla Catalunya, 26, 08007 Barcelona, Spain
Facilities and Amenities: Free High-Speed Internet (WiFi), Rooftop pool, Fitness Center with Gym / Workout Room, Bar /

Lounge, Babysitting services, Pets allowed (Dog / Pet Friendly), Room service, Safe in rooms, VIP room facilities, Non-smoking rooms, Suites, Family rooms, Multilingual staff (English, French, Spanish, Catalan)

Dining Options: On-site restaurant and poolside bar

Price Range: $260 - $433 based on average rates for a standard room

Booking Information: Booking available through the hotel's official website and booking platforms like Booking.com.

Nearby Attractions: Casa Batlló, Passeig de Gràcia, La Rambla, restaurants, shops, and cultural attractions.

Safety and Accessibility: Security measures in place. Hotel is centrally located and accessible to nearby attractions.

Pet-Friendly Policy: Pets are allowed (Dog / Pet Friendly).

Environmental Practices: NH Hotel holds the "GreenLeaders Silver level" indicating its commitment to environmental practices.

5 BEST LUXURY LODGING RECOMMENDATION

1. W BARCELONA

W Barcelona is a luxurious 5-star hotel located on the beachfront along the famous Barceloneta Boardwalk. It offers a combination of luxury and comfort with stunning views over the Mediterranean Sea and the city of Barcelona.

Address: Placa Rosa del Vents, 1 Final Passeig de Joan de Borbo, 08039 Barcelona, Spain

Facilities and Amenities: The hotel offers valet parking, free high-speed internet (WiFi), pool, fitness center, bar/lounge, beach access, evening entertainment, and more. Room features include blackout curtains, bathrobes, air conditioning, minibar, flatscreen TV, and more.

Dining options: The Fire restaurant and the Eclipse rooftop bar.

Reviews and Ratings: The hotel has received 8,152 reviews on TripAdvisor with an overall rating of 4.0. It is ranked #313 out of 549 hotels in Barcelona.

Price range: $371 - $660 (Based on Average Rates for a Standard Room)

Booking information: Booking.com.

Nearby Attractions: Plaja de Sant Sebastian (beach), Eclipse (rooftop bar), and SUP&Sun Barcelona (water sports).

Pet-friendly policy: The hotel is pet-friendly (dogs/pets allowed).

Environmental practices: The hotel has achieved GreenLeaders Silver level for its environmental practices.

2. SERRAS BARCELONA

Serras Barcelona is a luxury boutique hotel located in the heart of Barcelona, Spain, offering a trendy and spacious accommodation experience with stunning views of the Mediterranean Sea. The hotel features a Michelin star Chef Restaurant, a rooftop terrace with an infinity pool, and personalized service.

Address: Passeig de Colom, 9, 08002 Barcelona, Spain

Facilities and Amenities: Rooftop bar, rooftop terrace with infinity pool, fitness center, free high-speed internet (WiFi), bar/lounge, airport transportation, allergy-free rooms, air conditioning, desk, coffee/tea maker, cable/satellite TV, bridal suite, non-smoking rooms, suites.

Dining options: The hotel offers a Michelin star Chef Restaurant and a rooftop terrace with Mediterranean tapas.

Reviews and Ratings: The hotel has received excellent reviews with a Travelers' Choice 2023 Winner award. It has a rating of 5.0 based on 1,932 reviews on TripAdvisor.

Price range: $396 - $884 based on Average Rates for a Standard Room

Booking information: Reservations can be made through the hotel's official website or through booking platforms like Booking.com.

Nearby Attractions: Gothic Quarter (Barri Gotic), Basílica de Santa Maria del Mar, and Handmade Barcelona.

Safety and Accessibility: The hotel offers paid public parking nearby and secured parking. The staff is known for their attentive service and helpfulness.

3. MAJESTIC HOTEL & SPA BARCELONA

Deluxe 5-star traditional hotel in the heart of Barcelona, located near Gaudi monuments and famous Rambla. Offers excellence in service, rooftop terrace with panoramic views, and outdoor pool.

Address: Passeig de Gracia 68, 08007 Barcelona, Spain

Facilities and Amenities: Paid private parking nearby, Free High-Speed Internet (WiFi), Pool, Fitness Center, Bar/lounge, Babysitting, Airport transportation, Business Center, Air conditioning, Housekeeping, Private balcony, Room service, Safe, Minibar, Refrigerator, Flatscreen TV

Dining Options: Rooftop bar, On-site restaurant, Lounge

Reviews and Ratings: 4.5 (Excellent) based on 3,748 reviews. Ranked #73 out of 549 hotels in Barcelona. GreenLeaders Silver level.

Price Range: $335 - $447 (Average Rates for a Standard Room)

Booking Information: Available through the hotel's official website: https://www.guestreservations.com/majestic-hotel-spa-barcelona/booking or various booking platforms including bookings.com, kayak.com

Nearby Attractions: Passeig de Gracia, Casa Batlló, Casa Milà - La Pedrera, Despacio Spa at The One

Safety and Accessibility: Security service, Rooftop terrace with city views, Close to attractions and restaurants

4. ME BARCELONA

ME Barcelona is a stylish and elegant *hotel* located in the heart of Barcelona. It offers modern accommodations, exceptional dining options, and a rooftop pool with stunning city views.

Address: Carrer Casp 1-13, 08010 Barcelona, Spain

Facilities and Amenities: The hotel features a pool with a view, yoga classes, a coffee shop, electric vehicle charging station, free internet, soundproof rooms, air conditioning, housekeeping, cable/satellite TV, and more. The hotel offers various room types including city view and landmark view rooms.

Dining Options: The hotel has several dining options including the BELBO Fasto, Terrenal, and Luma restaurants, where guests can enjoy exceptional food and drinks.

Reviews and Ratings: The hotel has received excellent reviews, with guests praising the beautiful design, attentive staff, comfortable rooms, rooftop pool, and great location.

Price Range: $394 to $609 for a standard room.

Booking Information: Guests can book directly on the hotel's website or through various booking platforms.

Nearby Attractions: Aventurico Barcelona, Arte Bar: Painting and Wine, Plaza de Toros Monumental de Barcelona, Bar La Higuera

Safety and Accessibility: The hotel offers reduced mobility rooms and facilities for disabled guests..

Pet-Friendly Policy: The hotel is pet-friendly, allowing dogs and pets to stay.

5. HOTEL EL PALACE BARCELONA

Hotel El Palace Barcelona is a luxurious and historic hotel located in the heart of Barcelona. The hotel offers a blend of classic elegance and modern amenities, providing guests with a comfortable and opulent stay experience.

Address: Gran Via de les Corts Catalanes, 668, 08010 Barcelona, Spain

Facilities and Amenities: The hotel offers various amenities including a rooftop bar, fitness center with gym, hot tub, business center, free high-speed internet (WiFi), room service, private balconies, safe, minibar, allergy-free rooms, air conditioning, and more.

Dining Options: The hotel features a rooftop restaurant and other dining options.

Reviews and Ratings: The hotel has received excellent reviews, with many guests praising the exceptional service, luxurious accommodations, & convenient location.

Price Range: $398 - $671 based on average rates for a standard room

Booking Information: Bookings can be made through the hotel's official website or various online booking platforms.

Nearby Attractions: The hotel is conveniently located near attractions such as Maximum Escape game centers and Museo Banksy - Barcelona.

Safety and Accessibility: The hotel provides information about its safety measures and is accessible to guests.

CHAPTER 5: BARCELONA'S NIGHTLIFE & ENTERTAINMENT SCENE

Welcome to the vibrant and exhilarating nightlife of Barcelona – a city that truly comes alive after the sun sets! Barcelona truly knows how to light up the night with its exuberant nightlife scene, catering to a diverse range of preferences – from relaxed hangouts to lively clubs.

9 BEST PLACES TO VISIT FOR A NIGHT OUT IN BARCELONA

You can embark on an unforgettable night out in Barcelona by exploring some of the best places to go for a night out in Barcelona below:

1. Razzmatazz: A giant among clubs, Razzmatazz is a hotspot that draws all sorts of enthusiasts. With five distinct rooms, each boasting its unique musical vibe, you're bound to discover the perfect rhythm for your night.

2. Pacha Barcelona: This legendary club has stood the test of time for over four decades, offering a high-octane atmosphere fueled by world-renowned DJs and pulsating beats.

3. Sutton Club: Delve into the underground charm of Sutton Club, where the fusion of house, techno, and electronica creates an irresistible dance haven.

4. Otto Zutz: For those seeking an unapologetically wild experience, Otto Zutz beckons with its uninhibited parties and carefree aura.

5. Moog: Moog sets a more mellow tone, inviting you to unwind and appreciate good music while sipping a drink. The eclectic mix of indie, rock, and electronica will resonate with your musical sensibilities.

6. Salamanca: A haven for house and techno aficionados.

7. Privilege: Noted for its capacious setting and rooftop terrace.

8. Macarena: Revered for its pulsating Latin rhythms and dynamic ambiance.

9. Luz de Gas: A hotspot for jazz and blues enthusiasts.

In Barcelona, a plethora of options await those seeking

bars to unwind in, ranging from traditional tapas joints to trendy cocktail lounges. The city hosts an array of renowned establishments, including:

Boadas: Famed for its timeless cocktails and Art Deco ambiance.
Opium Barcelona: Distinguished by its electronic beats and exclusive VIP sections.
Bar Marsella: One of the city's oldest bars, cherished by both locals and visitors.
La Bodega del Raval: A lively tapas haven celebrated for its delectable cuisine and vibrant atmosphere.
El Tibidabo: A favorite destination for sunset beverages, boasting breathtaking city vistas.

In the realm of live music, Barcelona offers a dynamic array of venues, showcasing various genres to suit every preference. Prominent live music venues include:

Sala Apolo: Hosting a spectrum of concerts, from indie rock to electronica.
Sala Bikini: Presenting an array of pop and rock performances.
Jamboree: A bastion of jazz and blues melodies.
Liceu: Barcelona's premier opera house, featuring operas, ballets, and concerts.
Auditori: A concert hall hosting diverse classical music recitals.

Flamenco aficionados (individuals who are passionate or devoted enthusiasts of flamenco, a traditional art form originating in the Andalusian region of Spain) will find Barcelona's lively scene captivating, with notable shows such as:

Tablao Flamenco Carmen: An authentic flamenco spectacle in an enchanting tablao setting.

Tablao Flamenco Cordobes: Another traditional flamenco presentation set in an exquisite tablao environment.

La Cubana: A theater company offering a range of captivating Catalan productions, including musicals and comedies.

La Fura dels Baus: Recognized for avant-garde and visually striking theater performances.

Teatro del Liceu: Barcelona's premier opera house, hosting a diverse array of shows, from plays to musicals.

9 NIGHT ACTIVITIES TO INDULGE IN WHILE IN BARCELONA

1. Tapas and Drinks: Your night can start with a leisurely exploration of the city's tapas bars. Dive into the local culinary scene by indulging in small, flavorful dishes that range from traditional Spanish to avant-garde creations. Pair these delights with some of Spain's finest wines, vermouth, or innovative cocktails.

2. Beachfront Vibes: For a more relaxed evening, head to the beachfront bars and chiringuitos (beachside bars) that dot the coastline. With the sound of the waves in the background, enjoy a refreshing cocktail or a cold beer while watching the sunset over the Mediterranean Sea.

3. La Rambla and Gothic Quarter: The iconic La Rambla boulevard transforms at night, becoming a hub of activity with street performers, open-air concerts, and bustling bars. Nearby, the Gothic Quarter's narrow alleys lead you to hidden gems – cozy bars, jazz clubs, and flamenco shows that offer an intimate glimpse into Spain's rich cultural heritage.

4. Live Music: Music lovers are in for a treat with the city's thriving live music scene. From classic flamenco performances to rock concerts, jazz ensembles, and electronic music events, Barcelona caters to every musical taste. Check out venues like Razzmatazz, Apolo, and Palau de la Música for unforgettable performances.

5. Dance the Night Away: Barcelona is renowned for its electrifying dance floors. The city's clubs are internationally acclaimed, offering a variety of electronic music genres that keep the party going until the early hours. Pacha Barcelona, Opium, and Sutton Club are just a few of the top names in the scene.

6. Rooftop Bars: Elevate your nightlife experience by sipping cocktails at one of Barcelona's numerous rooftop bars. These panoramic venues offer breathtaking views of the city skyline, making for a perfect setting to socialize, unwind, and enjoy the cool evening breeze.

7. Flamenco Shows: Immerse yourself in Spain's passionate and soul-stirring dance form, flamenco. Several venues in Barcelona offer live flamenco performances that captivate audiences with their powerful rhythms, heartfelt melodies, and intricate footwork.

8. La Boqueria Night Market: Indulge in a unique experience at La Boqueria, one of Europe's most famous food markets. On certain evenings, the market transforms into a vibrant night market, where you can sample a wide array of culinary delights and join locals in enjoying a casual evening out.

9. Late-Night Dining: Craving a midnight snack? Barcelona's late-night dining scene has you covered. From traditional Spanish late-night eateries to international cuisine, you can satisfy your hunger at any hour.

Barcelona's nightlife is a reflection of its diverse culture and people. Be sure to immerse yourself in the atmosphere, respect local customs, and embrace the energy that comes with the city's after-dark scene.

HANDY TIPS TO ENJOY THE BEST OF NIGHTLIFE IN BARCELONA

Weekend Wonders: The weekends are prime time for the liveliest club experiences.

Budget-Friendly Options: Keep an eye out for budget-friendly or free events happening throughout the week.

Dress the Part: Elevate your experience by adhering to the club's dress code, ensuring you fit right in.

Stay Aware: Stay vigilant against pickpockets and be mindful of your surroundings.

Unleash Your Spirit: Let loose and revel in the city's innate party spirit – after all, Barcelona knows how to celebrate!

CHAPTER 6: SHOPPING AND SOUVENIRS IN BARCELONA

Barcelona is not only known for its stunning architecture and vibrant culture, but also for its diverse shopping scene and unique souvenirs. In this chapter, we'll explore the different shopping districts and streets, discover local crafts and artisans, and find out where to acquire those one-of-a-kind souvenirs.

SHOPPING DISTRICTS AND STREETS

Barcelona boasts a wide range of shopping districts and streets that cater to various preferences and budgets. Here are a few notable ones:

1. Passeig de Gràcia: This upscale avenue is home to some of the world's most renowned luxury brands and designer boutiques. It's also where you'll find iconic architectural works like Gaudí's Casa Batlló and La Pedrera.

2. Portal de l'Àngel: If you're looking for more mainstream shopping, this pedestrian street is lined with popular high-street stores, making it a great spot for fashion and accessories.

3. El Raval: This neighborhood is known for its alternative and eclectic shops, selling everything from vintage clothing to quirky homeware. It's a hub for independent designers and unique finds.

4. Gràcia: Offering a bohemian atmosphere, the Gràcia district is home to many local artisan shops, showcasing handmade jewelry, clothing, and crafts.

5. El Born: This medieval neighborhood is filled with small shops selling artisanal goods, antiques, and unique jewelry. It's a perfect place to explore narrow streets and hidden treasures.

LOCAL CRAFTS AND ARTISANS

Barcelona is rich with local craftsmanship, and you can find unique handmade items that truly reflect the city's culture and history. Here are some examples of local crafts and artisans to look out for:

1. Ceramics: Traditional Catalan ceramics are renowned for their intricate designs and vibrant colors. Look for hand-painted plates, tiles, and decorative objects.

2. Espadrilles: These traditional woven shoes are not only comfortable but also fashionable. Many local shops offer a variety of espadrilles, often handcrafted and adorned with creative designs.

3. Textiles: Barcelona is known for its high-quality textiles, including delicate lacework and colorful textiles used in traditional outfits.

4. Glasswork: Skilled glassblowers produce exquisite glass pieces, ranging from intricate glass mosaics to delicate glassware.

5. Leather Goods: Local artisans create beautifully crafted leather goods, such as bags, belts, and wallets. Look for shops that prioritize quality materials and craftsmanship.

WHERE TO FIND UNIQUE SOUVENIRS

When searching for souvenirs that stand out from the typical tourist fare, consider these options:

1. Mercat de la Boqueria: This bustling food market is also a great place to find local delicacies, such as spices, olive oil, and traditional sweets, which make for unique edible souvenirs.

2. Craft Markets: Keep an eye out for craft fairs and markets that pop up around the city. These events showcase the work of local artisans and offer a chance to buy directly from the creators.

3. Artisan Shops: Explore the neighborhoods mentioned earlier for boutique stores specializing in locally made crafts, clothing, and accessories.

4. Museums and Cultural Centers: Many museums and cultural centers have gift shops selling items related to their exhibitions, providing an opportunity to bring home pieces inspired by art and history.

Keep in mind that when shopping for souvenirs, it's a good idea to support local artisans and sustainable practices whenever possible. This not only ensures the authenticity of the items but also contributes to the preservation of Barcelona's unique cultural heritage.

CHAPTER 7: BEYOND BARCELONA: TOP 10 DAY TRIPS FROM BARCELONA

While you could spend weeks exploring the various neighborhoods of Barcelona, there's always more to discover – from trying local cuisine to visiting bars and uncovering hidden gems. But to experience the authentic Catalan lifestyle beyond the city or to simply switch up the pace, embark on a day trip from Barcelona to discover the charm of nearby mountains, beaches, and picturesque towns. Below is our selection of the Top 10 short getaways from the captivating city of Barcelona.

MONTSERRAT

Montserrat, 60 km (37 mi) northwest of Barcelona, Spain, boasts scenic beauty, the Montserrat monastery, and hiking trails.

OVERVIEW

A UNESCO World Heritage Site, Montserrat houses the Santa Maria de Montserrat Benedictine monastery, founded in the 11th century. The monastery draws pilgrims to its Black Madonna statue, believed to possess miraculous powers. Hiking and rock climbing are popular activities, with trails of various difficulty levels.

GETTING TO MONTSERRAT

Train: Take the R5 train from Plaça de Catalunya to Montserrat-Aeri station (1.5 hrs).

Bus: Buses from Plaça d'Espanya to Montserrat-Manresa bus station (1 hr 15 min).

Car: Drive via AP-7 motorway, exiting at Montserrat-Manresa (1 hr 15 min).

MONTSERRAT MUST-SEE AND DO

Montserrat Monastery: Complex with museum, library, and basilica housing the revered Black Madonna.

Santa Cova Chapel: Short hike from the monastery to the chapel, believed to mark where the Black Madonna was discovered.

Hiking: Explore varying difficulty trails to summit, offering stunning vistas.

Santa Cova: Visit the cave where the Black Madonna was found.

Cable Car/Rack Railway: Swift ascents with cable car or scenic rack railway options.

Enjoy Views: Savor breathtaking mountain and surrounding views.

Montserrat Museum: Discover an impressive art collection including works by Picasso, El Greco, and Dalí

Santa Maria de Montserrat Abbey: A Benedictine retreat with stunning architecture and panoramic views, perfect for reflection.

COLLSEROLA

Collserola, north of Barcelona, Spain, is part of the Catalan Coastal Range, offering hiking, biking, and picnicking. The highest peak, Tibidabo, reaches 512 meters (1,680 feet).

TRAVEL TIME FROM BARCELONA

Car: About 20 minutes to park entrance.
Public Transportation: 30 minutes by FGC train & Funicular de Vallvidrera

GETTING TO COLLSEROLA

Car: Use A2 motorway, exit at Sant Cugat del Vallès, follow signs.
Public Transportation: Take FGC train to Peu del Funicular, then take Funicular de Vallvidrera to Collserola.
Bike: Follow bike trails or rent one in Barcelona.

THINGS TO SEE AND DO IN COLLSEROLA

Hike/Bike Trails: Explore varying trails, leading to Tibidabo's peak with panoramic Barcelona views.

Tibidabo Amusement Park: Family-friendly attraction atop Tibidabo.

Torre de Collserola: Telecommunications tower offering stunning Barcelona views.

Picnic Areas: Enjoy open-air meals at designated spots.

Sant Cugat del Vallès Monastery:** Beautiful complex with museum and library, located at the foot of Collserola.

Stargazing: Escape city lights for optimal stargazing experiences.

GIRONA

Nestled in northeastern Spain within the Catalonia region, Girona stands as a captivating city renowned for its medieval allure. The picturesque landscape is adorned with the remnants of a bygone era, including the well-preserved walled Old Quarter, the Roman vestiges of the Força Vella fortress, and an extraordinary Jewish Quarter, among other gems.

Travel time from Barcelona: 1 hour and 15 minutes
Getting to Girona: Catch the train every 30 minutes from Barcelona. A one-way trip on the fast train costs around €16 and takes just 40 minutes.

GIRONA MUST-SEE AND DO

Embark on a Journey through Time in the Old Quarter (Barri Vell): Girona's heart beats within its historic Old Quarter. Here, you can discover landmarks like the Girona Cathedral, the intricate Jewish Quarter, and enduring Roman walls.
Intricate Exploration of the Jewish Quarter: Among Europe's

most impeccably preserved Jewish Quarters, this labyrinth of narrow lanes and alleys resides within the Old Quarter.

Scenic Strolls along the Passeig Arqueològic: Walking the medieval ramparts of the Old Quarter, the Passeig Arqueològic offers breathtaking city panoramas and views of the meandering River Onyar.

Awe-Inspiring Visit to the Cathedral of Girona: Graceful Gothic architecture defines the grandeur of the Girona Cathedral, one of Spain's largest. Enveloped by the Old Quarter, the cathedral beckons every Girona explorer.

Time Travel through the Roman Ruins of Força Vella: Explore the Roman remains of Força Vella in the Old Quarter. These ruins provide captivating views of the city and the peaceful River Onyar.

Retail Therapy in Old Quarter's Boutiques: The charming Old Quarter plays host to a medley of shops and boutiques, where treasured souvenirs, gifts, and apparel await discovery.

Culinary Delights at Old Quarter Restaurants: Savor the diverse flavors of Catalan cuisine at the array of restaurants scattered throughout the Old Quarter.

FIGUERES

Figueres, located around 137 kilometers (85 miles) north of Barcelona is renowned as the birthplace of surrealist artist Salvador Dalí. The town boasts the Salvador Dalí Theater-Museum, a highly frequented museum within Spain.

Travel Time from Barcelona: 1 hour and 15 minutes. Renfe and FGC are a couple of the train companies providing service to Figueres. Trains set off from Barcelona's Sants station and reach Figueres Vilafant station.

REACHING FIGUERES

By Train: Board the R11 train from Barcelona's Sants station to Figueres Vilafant station, with a travel time of approximately 1 hour and 15 minutes.

By Bus: Several bus companies, such as Sarfa and Moventis, run routes to Figueres. Buses depart from Barcelona's Nord station and arrive at Figueres bus station, taking around 1 hour and 45 minutes.

By Car: Driving from Barcelona to Figueres takes approximately

1 hour and 30 minutes. Optimal route involves taking the AP-7 motorway and exiting at Figueres.

THINGS TO SEE AND DO IN FIGUERES

Salvador Dalí Theater-Museum: A must-visit for Dalí enthusiasts, this museum showcases an extensive collection of his artworks, encompassing paintings, sculptures, and drawings.

Exploration of the Old Town: Figueres' medieval old town boasts narrow streets and vibrant houses. Noteworthy landmarks include the Church of Sant Pere and the Gothic Palace of the Counts of Empúries.

Stroll through Parc de la Ciutadella: This central park provides a serene outdoor setting with gardens, fountains, and sculptures.

Savor Local Cuisine: Figueres is home to exceptional restaurants serving traditional Catalan fare. Delight in dishes like escalivada, roasted vegetables, or arròs negre, squid ink-infused rice.

SITGES

Situated along the Catalonia coast, Sitges beckons as a picturesque town located around 30 kilometers (19 miles) to the south of Barcelona. Known for its stunning beaches, lively nightlife, and creative ambiance, Sitges offers a unique coastal experience.

Travel Time from Barcelona: approximately 30 minutes. Renfe and FGC

HOW TO REACH SITGES

By Train: Board the R2S train at Barcelona's Passeig de Gràcia station, reaching Sitges train station in around 30 minutes.

By Bus: Various bus companies, such as Sarfa and Moventis, connect Barcelona's Nord station to Sitges bus station in about 45 minutes.

By Car: The drive from Barcelona to Sitges takes roughly 30 minutes.

THINGS TO SEE AND DO SITGES

Beachside Retreat: Enjoy the allure of Sitges' exquisite beaches, offering ideal settings for swimming, sunbathing, and surfing.

Discovery of the Old Town: Wander through the enchanting medieval streets of Sitges' old town. Admire its narrow alleys and vibrant houses, with notable landmarks such as the Church of Sant Bartomeu and the Sitges Museum.

Promenade Strolls: The promenade provides splendid views of the Mediterranean Sea and marina yachts. Discover an array of restaurants and bars nestled along this inviting pathway.

Cau Ferrat Museum Exploration: Immerse yourself in the Cau Ferrat Museum's collection, featuring artworks and artifacts by prominent Catalan artists like Santiago Rusiñol and Ramón Casas.

Nightlife Indulgence: As the sun sets, Sitges comes alive with its vibrant nightlife scene. Experience the energetic atmosphere of bars and clubs that keep their doors open well into the night.

VILANOVA I LA GELTRU

Vilanova i la Geltrú stands proudly around 40 kilometers (25 miles) south of Barcelona. With its roots tracing back to Roman times, this port city boasts a rich history. Known for its pristine beaches, thriving cultural landscape, and delectable cuisine, Vilanova i la Geltrú offers a multifaceted experience.

Travel Time from Barcelona: 45 minutes

GETTING TO VILANOVA I LA GELTRÚ

By Train: Embark on the R2S train from Barcelona's Passeig de Gràcia station, culminating in Vilanova i la Geltrú train station within 45 minutes.

By Bus: Numerous bus operators, such as Sarfa and Moventis, link Barcelona's Nord station to Vilanova i la Geltrú bus station in approximately 1 hour.

By Car: A drive from Barcelona to Vilanova i la Geltrú takes roughly 45 minutes, with the C32 motorway being the recommended route.

THINGS TO SEE AND DO IN VILLANOVA

Beachside Bliss: Bask in the allure of Vilanova i la Geltrú's stunning beaches, offering idyllic settings for swimming, sunbathing, and surfing.

Journey Through the Old Town: Stroll through the captivating medieval streets of Vilanova i la Geltrú's old town. Admire the narrow lanes and vibrant houses, while discovering historical treasures like the Church of Sant Antoni Abat and the Vilanova i la Geltrú Museum.

Promenade Serenity: Delight in mesmerizing views of the Mediterranean Sea and marina yachts while traversing the promenade. Indulge in the culinary offerings of the various restaurants & bars lining this pathway.

Museu del Ferrocarril Exploration: Immerse yourself in the Museu del Ferrocarril, which houses an assortment of railway artifacts, including locomotives, carriages, and signaling equipment.

Vibrant Nightlife: As twilight descends, Vilanova i la Geltrú comes alive with its spirited nightlife. Experience the energetic ambiance of bars and clubs that remain open well into the night.

TARRAGONA

Tarragona, nestled in Catalonia, Spain, stands about 100 kilometers (62 miles) to the south of Barcelona. As a port city with an illustrious history dating back to the Roman era, Tarragona boasts remarkably preserved Roman ruins, picturesque beaches, and delectable culinary offerings.

Travel Time from Barcelona: 1 hour and 30 minutes

Getting to Tarragona

By Train: Board the R16 train at Barcelona's Sants station, arriving at Tarragona station after about 1 hour and 30 minutes.

By Bus: Various bus operators, including Sarfa and Moventis, link Barcelona's Nord station to Tarragona bus station in roughly 1 hour and 45 minutes.

By Car: The drive from Barcelona to Tarragona takes about 1 hour and 30 minutes, with the AP-7 motorway being the recommended route.

THINGS TO SEE AND DO IN TARRAGONA

Roman Amphitheatre Exploration: Witness one of the world's best-preserved Roman amphitheaters. Constructed in the 2nd century AD, it could accommodate up to 20,000 spectators.

Journey Through the Old Town: Traverse the captivating medieval alleys of Tarragona's old town. Admire narrow streets and vibrant houses, uncovering historical treasures like the Tarragona Cathedral and the El Serrallo neighborhood.

Stroll Down Rambla Nova: Tarragona's central street, Rambla Nova, offers an excellent setting for people-watching while soaking in views of the Mediterranean Sea.

Tarraco Museum Exploration: Immerse yourself in the Tarraco Museum, housing an array of artifacts from Tarragona's Roman heritage, including sculptures, mosaics, and pottery.

Beachside Bliss: Experience Tarragona's beautiful beaches, offering an ideal backdrop for swimming, sunbathing, and surfing.

MONT BLANC

Mont Blanc, a sizable medieval walled town stands as the loftiest peak in the Alps and all of Western Europe. Situated on the border between France and Italy, this majestic mountain attracts enthusiasts of mountaineering, hiking, and skiing. Montblanc offers a range of dining and lodging options. While worth a visit on its own merits, the town is best explored with a car, allowing you to fully engage with the Cistercian Route, featuring three stunning monasteries in close proximity: Poblet, Vallbona de les Monges, and Santes Creues. To visit all three, an early start is recommended.

Travel Duration from Barcelona: Driving takes around 6 hours to reach Chamonix, the quaint French town at the mountain's base. Taking the TGV train to Saint-Gervais-les-Bains and then a shuttle bus to Chamonix requires about 7 hours.

Getting to Mont Blanc
By car: Travel via the A2 motorway towards Perpignan, then

transition onto the A9 motorway leading to Chamonix.

By train: Board the TGV train from Barcelona toSaint-Gervais-les-Bains, later transitioning to a shuttle bus to reach Chamonix.

By bus: Several bus companies, such as FlixBus and Alsa, provide services to Chamonix.

THINGS TO SEE AND DO IN MONT BLANC

Ascend to Mont Blanc's summit on foot: **A** demanding hike suited for seasoned mountaineers.

Reach Mont Blanc's pinnacle via cable car: **A** less demanding option to relish the summit's panoramic vistas.

Engage in skiing or snowboarding

Visit the Mer de Glace glacier: **Explore** this glacier situated at Mont Blanc's foothills.

Roam through Chamonix and Courmayeur: **Situated** at the mountain's base, these towns offer dining, shopping, and nightlife options

COLÒNIA GÜELL

Colònia Güell, situated around 15 kilometers (9 miles) southwest of Barcelona in Santa Coloma de Cervelló, was once an industrial estate. Established in 1890 by Catalan industrialist Eusebi Güell, it aimed to create a model community for workers.

Architect Antoni Gaudí designed this estate, crafting key buildings like the Crypt, Church, and Colònia Güell School.

Travel Time from Barcelona: Roughly 20 minutes by train, 30 minutes by Bus.

Getting to Colònia Güell

By train: Board the R5 train at Barcelona's Plaça de Catalunya station, arriving at Colònia Güell station in approximately 20 minutes.

By bus: Bus services by companies like Sarfa and Moventis connect Barcelona's Plaça d'Espanya to Colònia Güell bus stop in around 30 minutes.

By car: The C-32 motorway's Santa Coloma de Cervelló exit leads to the 20-minute drive from Barcelona to Colònia Güell.

Things to See and Do at Colònia Güell

Explore the Crypt: Gaudí's sole finished work in Colònia Güell, the Crypt showcases his distinctive style.

Engage with the Church: While under construction, visitors can access the crypt and museum.

Discover the Colònia Güell School: Now a museum chronicling its history, the School stands as a splendid example of modernist architecture.

Stroll through the gardens: The meticulously landscaped gardens provide breathtaking countryside vistas.

VIC

Vic is a beautiful medieval city in Catalonia, Spain. It is the capital of the Osona comarca and is located about 69 kilometers from Barcelona. Vic is known for its well-preserved historic center, its many churches and monasteries, and its traditional Catalan cuisine.

How to Get to Vic

By car: Take the AP-7 highway north from Barcelona. Exit at Vic and follow the signs into the city center.
By train: Take the R3 train from Barcelona-Passeig de Gràcia station to Vic. The travel duration is approximately one hour and twenty minutes.
By bus: There are several bus companies that offer direct bus services between Barcelona and Vic. The travel duration is approximately one hour and thirty minutes.

Things to See and Do in Vic

- Visit the Cathedral of Vic. The cathedral was built in the 12th century and is one of the most important

examples of Romanesque architecture in Catalonia.
- Explore the old town. The old town of Vic is a maze of narrow streets and medieval buildings.
- Visit the Museu Episcopal de Vic. The museum houses a collection of Catalan art from the Romanesque and Gothic periods.
- Take a walk through the Parc de la Campa. The park is located in the heart of the city and offers stunning views of the surrounding mountains.
- Sample the local cuisine. Vic is known for its traditional Catalan cuisine, which includes dishes such as fuet (a dried pork sausage), botifarra (a pork sausage), and crema catalana (a custard tart).

SOME BEAUTIFUL MEDIEVAL VILLAGES IN CATALONIA YOU MIGHT CONSIDER VISITING

Castellar de n'Hug: Castellar de n'Hug is a medieval village in perched on a cliff overlooking the Llobregat River. Known for its 11th-century castle, it's a magnet for hikers and nature enthusiasts.

Besalú: a medieval town 100 kilometers from Barcelona, is a UNESCO World Heritage Site famous for well-preserved Romanesque architecture, including the Pont Vell (Old Bridge), Jewish Quarter, and Sant Pere Monastery.

Rupit, a medieval village 120 kilometers from Barcelona, Catalonia, boasts a dramatic cliffside perch overlooking the Rupit River. A magnet for hikers and nature enthusiasts.

Peratallada: Peratallada is a medieval village 130 kilometers from Barcelona, Catalonia, enchants visitors with its well-preserved walls and castle. A sought-after spot for couples and romantic getaways.Siurana, Catalonia, Spain, sits 150 km (93 mi) from Barcelona on a cliff above the Siurana River, attracting hikers and nature enthusiasts.:

Siurana: Nestled in Catalonia, Spain, Siurana captivates with its cliffside charm. Perched above the Siurana River, this village is 150 km (93 miles) from Barcelona. Hikers and nature lovers flock to explore panoramic vistas and invigorating trails.

Castellfollit de la Roca: Another Catalonia treasure, 110 km (68 miles) from Barcelona. This village perches on a basalt cliff overlooking the Fluvià River. Photographers adore its unique vantage points and play of light and shadow.

Monells: A charming medieval enclave, 130 km (81 miles) from Barcelona. Sant Pere Church and the Town Hall offer a nostalgic journey through time. Monells delights wine enthusiasts with historic streets and local flavors.

Sant Quirze de Besora: 100 km (62 miles) from bustling Barcelona. Impeccably preserved medieval castle and church reflect Catalonia's rich heritage. Hikers relish both natural beauty and cultural legacy.

Talamanca: 120 km (75 miles) from Barcelona, a realm of romance and antiquity. Encircled by medieval walls, the village boasts a fairy tale castle, perfect for couples seeking history's embrace.

Guimerà: Serenely resting 140 km (87 miles) from bustling Barcelona. This hilltop village overlooks the meandering Cinca River, offering hikers and nature enthusiasts an escape to Catalonia's wild heart.

These Catalonia destinations, with unique charms for nature lovers, photographers, wine enthusiasts, and couples, weave a tapestry of experiences that blend Spain's captivating past and present.

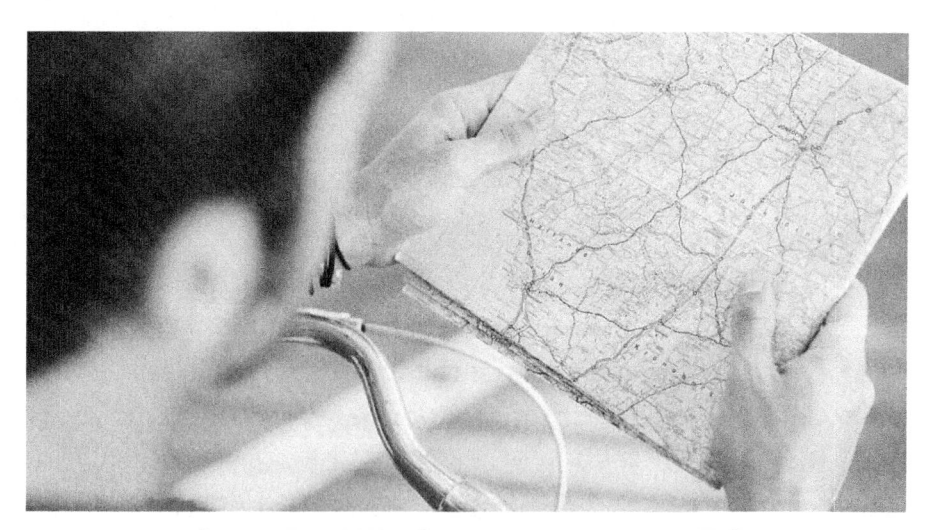

CHAPTER 8: ITINERARIES

ITINERARIES

5-HOURS BARCELONA ITINERARY

1. Explore the Gothic Quarter and Barcelona Cathedral (1 hour)
- Start your day in the heart of Barcelona's historic center, the Gothic Quarter.
- Wander through its narrow streets, admiring the medieval architecture and charming squares.
- Visit the Barcelona Cathedral (Catedral de Barcelona) known for its stunning Gothic design and intricate details.
- Take in the panoramic views of the city from the cathedral's rooftop.

2. Stroll along La Rambla and visit Mercado de La Boqueria (1.5 hours)
- Walk down La Rambla, one of Barcelona's most famous streets, lined with shops, cafes, and street performers.
- Stop at the vibrant Mercado de La Boqueria, a bustling food market, and indulge in fresh fruits, seafood, and local specialties.
- Experience the lively atmosphere and colors of the market.

3. Discover the artistic vibe of El Born and its cultural attractions (2.5 hours)
- Head to the El Born district, known for its artistic flair and historic sites.
- Visit the Picasso Museum to see an impressive collection of works by the renowned artist.
- Explore the medieval architecture of the area, which includes the Palau de la Música Catalana, a modernist concert hall.
- Take a leisurely stroll through Parc de la Ciutadella, a

green oasis in the heart of the city.

This itinerary provides a glimpse into Barcelona's rich history, art, and culinary scene within a short timeframe. Keep in mind that the walking times are approximate and may vary based on your pace and the time you spend at each location. Enjoy your 5-hour exploration of Barcelona!

1-DAY BARCELONA ITINERARY

Morning: Sagrada Familia and Park Güell
- Start your day with an early visit to the iconic Basilica of the Sagrada Familia, Antoni Gaudí's masterpiece.
- Marvel at the intricate facades and unique architecture of this still-in-progress basilica.
- Consider purchasing tickets in advance to skip the lines and have a more convenient experience.
- After the Sagrada Familia, head to Park Güell, another Gaudí gem. The park offers a surreal landscape and colorful mosaics.
- Take a leisurely stroll through the park's pathways, capturing picturesque views of the city below.
- Don't miss the famous dragon statue and the colorful mosaics at the main terrace.

Afternoon: Explore the Gothic Quarter and Cathedral
- Move towards the historic heart of Barcelona, the Gothic Quarter.
- Wander through the labyrinthine streets, discovering hidden squares and charming cafes.
- Explore the Barcelona Cathedral, a masterpiece of Gothic architecture. Climb to the top for panoramic city views.
- Take a break for lunch at a local cafe, savoring Catalan cuisine and tapas.

Evening: Enjoy dinner at a local restaurant and stroll along La Barceloneta beach
- In the evening, head to La Barceloneta, Barcelona's beach neighborhood.

- Choose a local seafood restaurant for dinner along the beachfront, enjoying the sea breeze and fresh catches.
- After dinner, take a relaxing stroll along the beach promenade. You can even dip your toes in the Mediterranean if weather permits.
- Alternatively, if you're interested in nightlife, you can explore the bars and clubs in the area to experience Barcelona's vibrant evening scene.

2-DAYS BARCELONA ITINERARY

DAY 1

Morning: Basilica of the Sagrada Familia
- Begin your first day with an early visit to the Basilica of the Sagrada Familia, one of the most iconic landmarks in Barcelona.
- Admire the intricate facades, towering spires, and the interior's awe-inspiring design.
- Learn about Gaudí's architectural vision and the history of the basilica through audio guides or guided tours.

Afternoon: Visit Casa Batlló and explore Eixample
- Head to Casa Batlló, another architectural marvel designed by Gaudí.
- Explore its whimsical interiors and fascinating design elements.
- After visiting Casa Batlló, take a stroll through the Eixample district, known for its unique grid pattern and modernist architecture.
- Stop for lunch at a local cafe or restaurant, enjoying the district's charming ambiance.

Evening: Relax at Park Güell
Spend your evening at Park Güell, another Gaudí creation known for its colorful mosaics and artistic design.
Take a leisurely walk through the park's landscaped gardens and enjoy panoramic views of the city.
Capture the sunset from one of the park's viewpoints before heading back to your accommodation.

DAY 2

<u>Morning: Explore the Gothic Quarter and Barcelona Cathedral</u>
- Begin your second day by immersing yourself in the historic charm of the Gothic Quarter.
- Visit the Barcelona Cathedral and consider climbing to the top for panoramic city views.
- Explore the narrow streets, discovering hidden gems, boutique shops, and local cafes.

<u>Afternoon: Discover Montjuïc and its attractions</u>
- Head to Montjuïc, a hill overlooking the city with a variety of attractions.
- Visit Montjuïc Castle for historical insights and stunning vistas.
- Explore the Magic Fountain of Montjuïc and enjoy its evening light and music show.

<u>Evening: Experience Barcelona's nightlife in El Raval or Gràcia</u>
As night falls, explore the vibrant nightlife scene of Barcelona.
- Choose either El Raval or Gràcia to experience the local bars, live music venues, and trendy cafes.
- Enjoy dinner at a local restaurant followed by drinks and entertainment in the chosen neighborhood.

This 2-day itinerary offers a mix of Barcelona's iconic landmarks, architectural wonders, historic districts, and vibrant nightlife. Adjust the pace based on your preferences and take the time to truly immerse yourself in the city's unique culture and atmosphere.

5-DAYS ITINERARY IN BARCELONA

DAY 1

Morning: Begin at Ciutadella Park and explore its surroundings.
Afternoon: Visit the Picasso Museum and Gothic Quarter.
Evening: Enjoy dinner in El Born.

DAY 2

Morning: Experience the architectural wonders of Gaudi – Sagrada Familia and Casa Batlló.
Afternoon: Discover Passeig de Gràcia and its shops.
Evening: Relax at Park Güell.

DAY 3

Day trip to Montserrat for natural beauty and spirituality.

DAY 4

Morning: Explore Montjuïc and its attractions.
Afternoon: Visit Museu Nacional d'Art de Catalunya and Joan Miro Foundation.
Evening: Attend a vibrant festival if available.

DAY 5

Morning: Visit Museu d'Historia de Barcelona - MUHBA.
Afternoon: Shopping along famous districts and streets.
Evening: Savor the local culinary scene.

7-DAYS ITINERARY OPTION 1

DAY 1: ARRIVAL AND INTRODUCTION TO BARCELONA

- Arrive in Barcelona, check into your chosen accommodation.
- Take a leisurely evening stroll along La Barceloneta beach.
- Enjoy a traditional Spanish dinner at a local beachfront restaurant.

DAY 2: EXPLORING HISTORIC DISTRICTS

- Start your day at the Gothic Quarter, visiting the Cathedral of Barcelona.
- Explore El Born's charming streets and visit the Picasso Museum.
- Afternoon visit to the Basilica of Santa Maria del Mar.
- Evening at the Magic Fountain of Montjuïc for the light and music show.

DAY 3: ARCHITECTURAL WONDERS

- Morning tour of Antoni Gaudí's masterpieces: Sagrada Familia and Casa Batlló.
- Afternoon visit to Park Güell for its unique architecture and panoramic views.
- Evening at Palau de la Música Catalana for a musical performance.

DAY 4: CULINARY DELIGHTS

- Morning visit to Mercado de La Boqueria for a taste of Barcelona's food scene.
- Afternoon cooking class to learn to prepare Catalan delicacies.
- Evening dine at a mid-range restaurant, savoring local flavors.

DAY 5: CULTURAL IMMERSION

- Explore museums: MNAC, Joan Miro Foundation, and Museu Maritim de Barcelona.
- Afternoon visit to Parc de Montjuic for its cultural attractions.
- Evening at a local tapas bar in El Raval.

DAY 6: SHOPPING AND RELAXATION

- Morning shopping along Plaça de Catalunya and Passeig de Gràcia.
- Afternoon visit to Ciutadella Park for a leisurely stroll.
- Evening entertainment at one of Barcelona's vibrant nightlife spots.

DAY 7: DAY TRIP TO MONTSERRAT

- Full-day excursion to Montserrat to explore the stunning mountain monastery.
- Return to Barcelona in the evening, enjoying a farewell dinner.

7-DAYS ITINERARY OPTION 2

DAY 1-3: EXPLORING BARCELONA

- Follow the same itinerary for Days 1 to 3 as outlined in the first option.

DAY 4: DAY TRIP TO GIRONA AND FIGUERES

- Full-day excursion to Girona to explore its medieval streets and historic sites.
- Visit the Salvador Dalí Theatre-Museum in Figueres.
- Return to Barcelona in the evening.

DAY 5: COASTAL GETAWAY

- Day trip to Sitges for its beautiful beaches and artistic atmosphere.
- Explore local galleries and relax by the sea.
- Return to Barcelona in the evening.

DAY 6: MONTSERRAT AND BEYOND

- Morning visit to Montserrat to explore the monastery and stunning views.
- Afternoon excursion to Colònia Güell to see Gaudí's crypt.
- Return to Barcelona for the evening.

DAY 7: EXPLORING MORE DAY TRIP OPTIONS

- Choose one of the following day trips: Collserola, Vilanova i la Geltrú, Tarragona, Montblanc.
- Explore the chosen destination's attractions.
- Return to Barcelona in the evening.

These itineraries are just suggestions and can be customized based on your preferences and interests. Make sure to consider opening hours, transportation schedules, and any events or festivals that might be happening during your visit.

CHAPTER 9: PRACTICAL RESOURCES ABOUT BARCELONA

When planning a trip to Barcelona, it's important to have access to practical resources to help you navigate the city, find information, and make the most of your visit. In this chapter we share some practical resources and websites that can be very helpful on your Barcelona visit.

VISA INFORMATION AND REQUIREMENTS

Before traveling to Barcelona, it's important to check the visa requirements for your country of residence. Here are some general guidelines:

European Union (EU) Citizens: Citizens of EU member states can travel to Barcelona with a valid passport or national identity card. You don't need a visa for stays lasting up to 90 days.

Schengen Area Countries: Citizens of non-EU countries that are part of the Schengen Area can also travel to Barcelona without a visa for stays up to 90 days. A valid passport is required.

Non-Schengen Area Countries: Citizens of non-Schengen Area countries may require a visa to enter Barcelona. Before traveling, it's crucial to verify the visa requirements tailored to your particular country of origin. Visa applications should be made well in advance of your trip.

It's always a good idea to check with the relevant embassy or consulate for the most up-to-date visa information and requirements.

Important Information you should Know

Language: The official languages of Barcelona are Catalan and Spanish. English is also commonly spoken in tourist areas
Currency: The official currency of Spain is the Euro (€).
ATMs: ATMs are widely available throughout Barcelona, and

most accept international cards. Check with your bank for potential fees.

Credit Cards: Major credit cards like Visa, MasterCard, and American Express are widely accepted in restaurants, shops, and hotels.

Tipping: Tipping is not obligatory, but leaving a small tip (around 5-10%) is appreciated in restaurants and for exceptional service.

BASICS USEFUL PHRASES IN BOTH CATALONIAN AND SPANISH

GREETINGS

Catalan
- Bon dia! (Good morning!)
- Bona tarda! (Good afternoon!)
- Bona nit! (Good night!)
- Hola! (Hello!)
- Com estàs? (How are you?)

Spanish
- Buenos días! (Good morning!)
- Buenas tardes! (Good afternoon!)
- Buenas noches! (Good night!)
- Hola! (Hello!)
- Cómo estás? (How are you?)

DIRECTIONS

Catalan
- On és...? (Where is...?)
- Com arribo a...? (How do I get to...?)
- A l'esquerra (On the left)
- A la dreta (On the right)
- Endavant (Straight ahead)

Spanish
- Dónde está...? (Where is...?)
- Cómo llego a...? (How do I get to...?)
- A la izquierda (On the left)
- A la derecha (On the right)
- Todo recto (Straight ahead)

ORDERING FOOD

Catalan
- Voldria una taula per a... (I would like a table for...)
- Què em recomaneu? (What do you recommend?)
- Voldria això, si us plau. (I would like this, please.)
- L'addició, si us plau. (The bill, please.)
- Una aigua, si us plau. (A water, please.)

Spanish
- Quisiera una mesa para... (I would like a table for...)
- Qué me recomienda? (What do you recommend?)
- Quisiera esto, por favor. (I would like this, please.)
- La cuenta, por favor. (The bill, please.)
- Un agua, por favor. (A water, please.)

ASKING FOR HELP

Catalan
- Em podeu ajudar? (Can you help me?)
- Necessito ajuda. (I need help.)
- No entenc. (I don't understand.)
- On és el bany? (Where is the restroom?)
- Puc trucar a un taxi? (Can I call a taxi?)

Spanish
- Puede ayudarme? (Can you help me?)
- Necesito ayuda. (I need help.)
- No entiendo. (I don't understand.)
- Dónde está el baño? (Where is the restroom?)
- Puedo llamar a un taxi? (Can I call a taxi?)

EXPRESSING GRATITUDE

Catalan
- Moltes gràcies! (Thank you very much!)
- Molt amable! (Very kind!)

- És molt apreciat. (It's much appreciated.)
- Gràcies per tot. (Thanks for everything.)
- Gràcies per la vostra ajuda. (Thank you for your help.)

Spanish
- Muchas gracias! (Thank you very much!)
- Muy amable! (Very kind!)
- Es muy apreciado. (It's much appreciated.)
- Gracias por todo. (Thanks for everything.)
- Gracias por su ayuda. (Thank you for your help.)

Feel free to use these phrases to help you communicate effectively while in Barcelona. Learning a few basic phrases can go a long way in making your trip more enjoyable and engaging with the locals.

ENSURING SAFETY AND WELL-BEING IN BARCELONA

Stay vigilant against pickpockets: Barcelona experiences a prevalent issue with pickpocketing, particularly in bustling locales like La Rambla and the metro. Safeguard your belongings closely and avoid letting them leave your sight.

Limit cash carry: It's prudent to carry only the necessary cash for the day, stowing the surplus in a secure spot, such as your hotel's safe.

Utilize concealed pockets or money belts: Employing a money belt or hidden pocket can safeguard your valuables, offering protection even in the event of pickpocketing.

Exercise caution at ATMs: Opt for ATMs situated in well-lit, public spaces. Remain alert to your surroundings and avoid distractions from strangers.

Nighttime precautions: Avoid solitary walks during the night. When venturing out after dark, consider utilizing taxis or public transportation.

Stay hydrated: Barcelona's climate often boasts hot and sunny conditions, necessitating ample hydration. Consume sufficient water throughout the day to stay well-hydrated.

Sun protection: Shield yourself from the sun's harmful rays by donning sunscreen, a hat, and sunglasses.

Recognize heat-related risks: Heat exhaustion and heat stroke are severe medical concerns that demand immediate attention. Familiarize yourself with their symptoms and seek medical aid if necessary.

Secure travel insurance: Acquiring travel insurance offers coverage for medical expenses, lost luggage, and unforeseen travel-related incidents.

MEDICAL ASSISTANCE

Hospital Clínic de Barcelona
Situated in the Eixample district, this renowned public hospital stands among Spain's finest. It boasts a specialized English-speaking department to accommodate international patients.
Address: Villarroel 170, 08036 Barcelona, Spain
Phone: +34 932 27 54 00

Hospital Universitari Vall d'Hebron
Located in the Vall d'Hebron district, this public hospital features a dedicated English-speaking unit to serve foreign visitors.
Address: Passeig de Vall d'Hebron 119-129, 08035 Barcelona, Spain
Phone: +34 933 39 70 00

Centro Médico Teknon
Nestled in the Diagonal district, this private hospital offers a 24-hour emergency room and an array of medical services, including English-speaking medical professionals.
Address:** Avenida Diagonal 664, 08034 Barcelona, Spain
Phone: +34 901 123 456

Clinica Sagrada Familia
Positioned in the Eixample district, this private clinic features a 24-hour emergency room and provides diverse medical services, including care from English-speaking doctors.
Address: Carrer Provença 238, 08037 Barcelona, Spain
Phone: +34 932 15 11 11

In the event of a medical emergency, you can dial 112, which is the universal European emergency number. This will connect you to local emergency services, enabling prompt dispatch of an ambulance or other necessary aid.

Furthermore, securing travel insurance prior to your trip to Barcelona is advisable. This insurance will cover potential medical expenses that may arise during your stay.

CONTACTING THE LOCAL POLICE (MOSSOS D'ESQUADRA)

The Barcelona local police is known as the ***Mossos d'Esquadra.***

Mossos d'Esquadra - Catalan Police Emergency Line: 112

The general emergency number in Spain, including Catalonia, is 112. You can dial this number for police, medical, and fire emergencies.

Non-Emergency Line: 088

The Mossos d'Esquadra have a non-emergency line for situations that do not require immediate attention. You can dial 088 to reach them.

Website: *https://mossos.gencat.cat/ca/inici*

The official website provides information about the police force, safety tips, and contact details.

Keep in mind that the Mossos d'Esquadra primarily operate in the Catalonia region, including Barcelona. For national-level police matters, you can also find the Policía Nacional and the Guardia Civil in Spain.

Please note that contact information may change over time, so it's a good idea to double-check the information before your trip.

RECOMMENDED TRAVEL APPS AND WEBSITES

PUBLIC TRANSPORTATION APPS

1. TMB App: The official app of Transports Metropolitans de Barcelona (TMB) provides real-time information on buses, trams, and the metro, including routes, schedules, and ticket prices.

2. Moovit: Moovit is a popular app that offers comprehensive public transportation information, including routes, schedules, and real-time updates for buses, trams, and the metro.

NAVIGATION

Google Maps: A versatile navigation app that offers walking, driving, and public transit directions. It can also show estimated travel times, traffic conditions, and alternative routes.

LANGUAGE APPS

1. *Duolingo:* A popular language learning app that offers quick lessons in various languages, including Catalan and Spanish.
2. **Memrise:** Another language learning app that focuses on vocabulary and phrases. It can be a handy tool for learning basic communication in local languages.

TOURIST INFORMATION APPS

1. *Barcelona Official Guide:* The official tourism app of Barcelona provides information about attractions, events, restaurants, and local recommendations.
2. *TripAdvisor:* While not exclusive to Barcelona,

TripAdvisor offers user reviews, ratings, and suggestions for accommodations, attractions, and dining options.

CURRENCY CONVERTER APPS

1. **_XE Currency:_** XE Currency is a reliable app for converting currencies. It provides real-time exchange rates and can work offline once rates are downloaded.

Remember to download and explore these apps before your trip to Barcelona for a smoother and more enjoyable experience. App availability and features may change over time, so make sure to check for the latest updates.

RECOMMENDED USEFUL WEBSITES

Official Barcelona Tourism Website: The official website of Barcelona's tourism board is an excellent resource for up-to-date information on attractions, events, accommodations, and practical travel tips. Visit: *https://www.barcelona.cat/en*

Barcelona Metro and Public Transportation: Barcelona's public transportation system, including the metro and buses, is efficient and well-connected. Check out TMB (Transports Metropolitans de Barcelona): *https://www.tmb.cat/en/home* for information on routes, tickets, and schedules.

Barcelona Card: The Barcelona Card offers discounts on public transportation, museums, attractions, and more. You can find details and purchase the card on the official Barcelona Card website: *https://www.barcelonacard.org*

Barcelona Airport: If you're arriving by air, the official website of Barcelona-El Prat Airport provides flight information, transportation options, and services available at the airport. Visit Barcelona Airport at *https://www.aena.es/en/josep-tarradellas-barcelona-el-prat.html*

Barcelona Weather: Check the weather forecast for Barcelona before your trip to help you plan accordingly. Websites like *https://weather.com* or AccuWeather: *https://www.accuweather.com* provide reliable weather updates.

Barcelona Accommodations: Websites like *Booking.com* and Airbnb can help you find a wide range of accommodation options, from hotels to apartments, hostels, and more.

Barcelona City Maps: Download or view maps of Barcelona to help you navigate the city. You can find maps on the official tourism website or use Google Maps for real-time navigation.

Barcelona Restaurant and Dining: Websites like *TripAdvisor.com* and *Yelp* offer user reviews and recommendations for restaurants and dining options in Barcelona.

Barcelona Events and Festivals: Check out websites like Time Out Barcelona: *https://www.timeout.com/barcelona* for information on upcoming events, festivals, concerts, and cultural happenings in the city.

MAPS

MAP 1: DISTRICTS OF BARCELONA
MAP 2: THE HARBOR AND CENTRAL AREA OF BARCELONA
MAP 3: A MORE DETAILED MAP OF BARCELONA
MAP 4: BARCELONA METRO MAP
MAP 5: PRINTABLE TOURIST MAP SHOWING THE MAIN ATTRACTIONS OF BARCELONA
MAP 6: NEIGHBORHOOD OF BARCELONA
MAP 7: LA RAMBLA PEDESTRIAN AVENUE
MAP 8: BARCELONA TOP 20 DESTINATIONS
MAP 9: BARCELONA TRAMWAY MAP

To get a zoomable PDF Format of the maps below, kindly send an email to: *theworldexplorergs@gmail.com*.

MAP 1: DISTRICTS OF BARCELONA

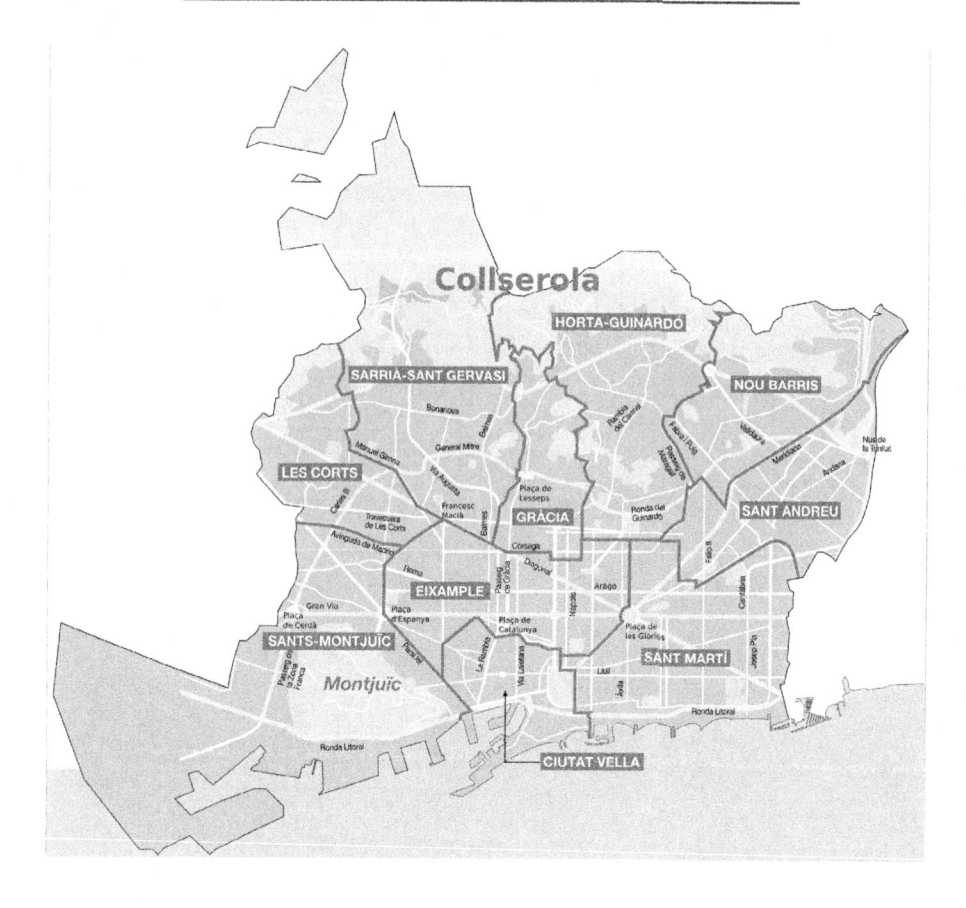

MAP 2: THE HARBOR AND CENTRAL AREA OF BARCELONA

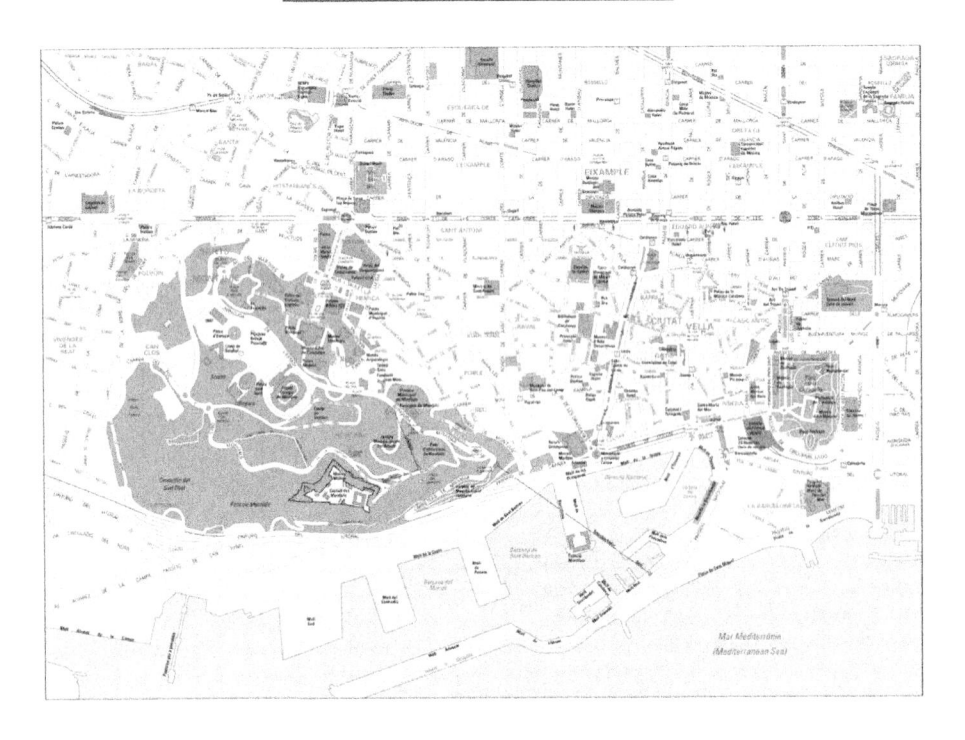

MAP 3: A MORE DETAILED MAP OF BARCELONA

MAP 4: BARCELONA METRO MAP

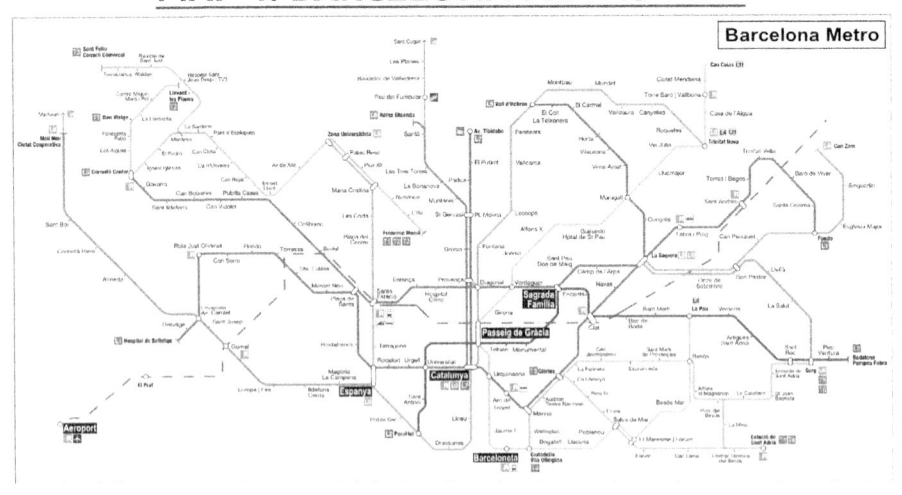

MAP 5: PRINTABLE TOURIST MAP SHOWING THE MAIN ATTRACTIONS OF BARCELONA

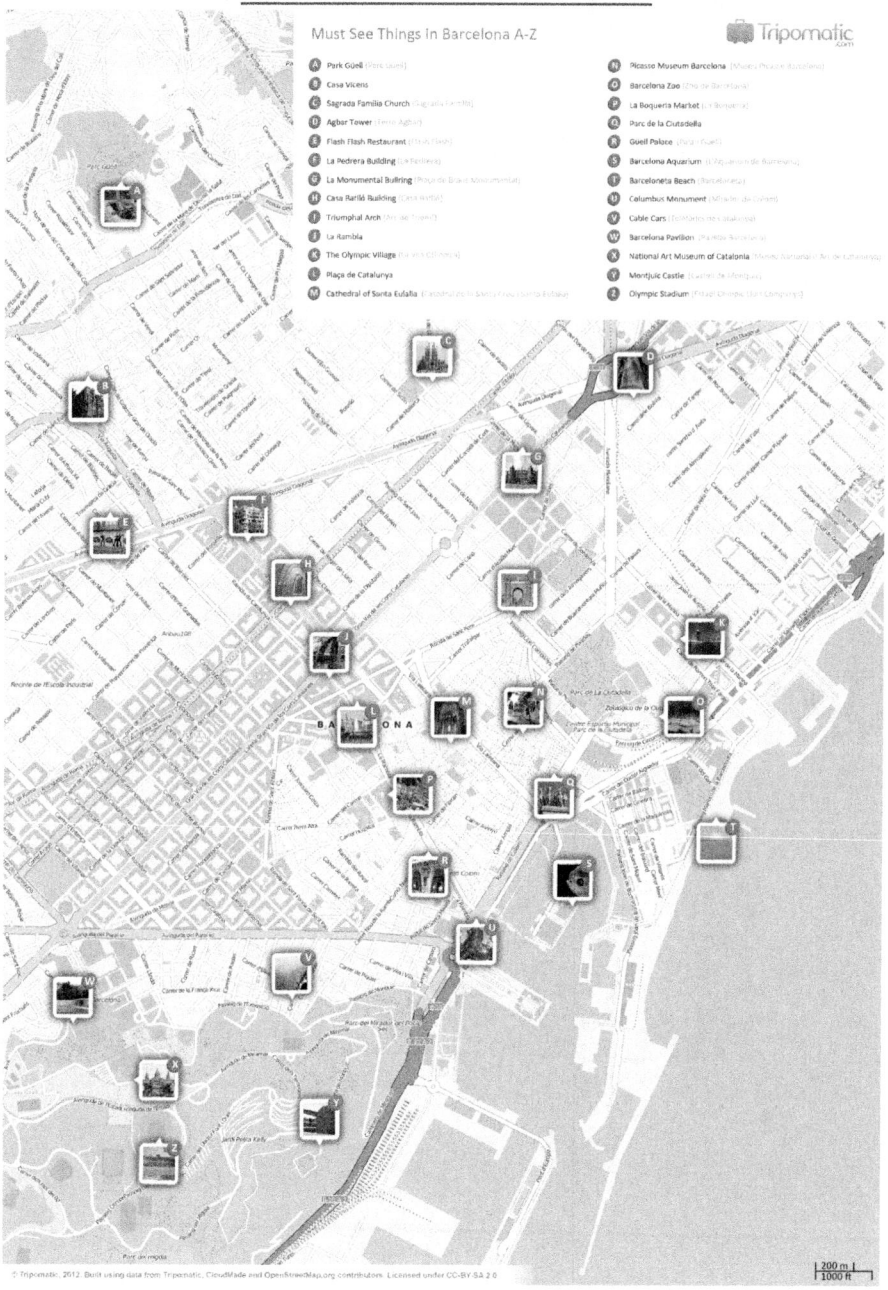

MAP 6: NEIGHBORHOOD OF BARCELONA

Ciutat Vella
1 el Raval
2 el Gòtic
3 la Barceloneta
4 Sant Pere, Santa Caterina i la Ribera

L'Eixample
5 el Fort Pienc
6 la Sagrada Família
7 la Dreta de l'Eixample
8 Antiga Esquerra de l'Eixample
9 Nova Esquerra de l'Eixample
10 Sant Antoni

Sants-Montjuïc
11 el Poble Sec
12 la Marina del Prat Vermell
13 la Marina de Port
14 la Font de la Guatlla
15 Hostafrancs
16 la Bordeta
17 Sants-Badal
18 Sants
PM Parc de Montjuïc
FP Zona Franca-Port

Les Corts
19 les Corts
20 la Maternitat i Sant Ramon
21 Pedralbes

Sarrià - Sant Gervasi
22 Vallvidrera, Tibidabo i les Planes
23 Sarrià
24 les Tres Torres
25 Sant Gervasi-Bonanova
26 Sant Gervasi-Galvany
27 el Putget i Farró

Gràcia
28 Vallcarca i els Penitents
29 el Coll
30 la Salut
31 Vila de Gràcia
32 el Camp d'en Grassot i Gràcia Nova

Horta - Guinardó
33 Baix Guinardó
34 Can Baró
35 el Guinardó
36 la Font d'en Fargues
37 el Carmel
38 la Teixonera
39 Sant Genís dels Agudells
40 Montbau
41 la Vall d'Hebron
42 la Clota
43 Horta

Nou Barris
44 Vilapicina-Torre Llobeta
45 Porta
46 el Turó de la Peira
47 Can Peguera
48 la Guineueta
49 Canyelles
50 les Roquetes
51 Verdun
52 la Prosperitat
53 la Trinitat Nova
54 Torre Baró
55 Ciutat Meridiana
56 Vallbona

Sant Andreu
57 la Trinitat Vella
58 Baró de Viver
59 el Bon Pastor
60 Sant Andreu
61 la Sagrera
62 el Congrés i els Indians
63 Navas

Sant Martí
64 el Camp de l'Arpa del Clot
65 el Clot
66 el Parc i la Llacuna del Poblenou
67 la Vila Olímpica del Poblenou
68 el Poblenou
69 Diagonal Mar i el Front Marítim del Poblenou
70 el Besòs i el Maresme
71 Provençals del Poblenou
72 Sant Martí de Provençals
73 la Verneda i la Pau

BARCELONA

MAP 7: LA RAMBLA PEDESTRIAN AVENUE

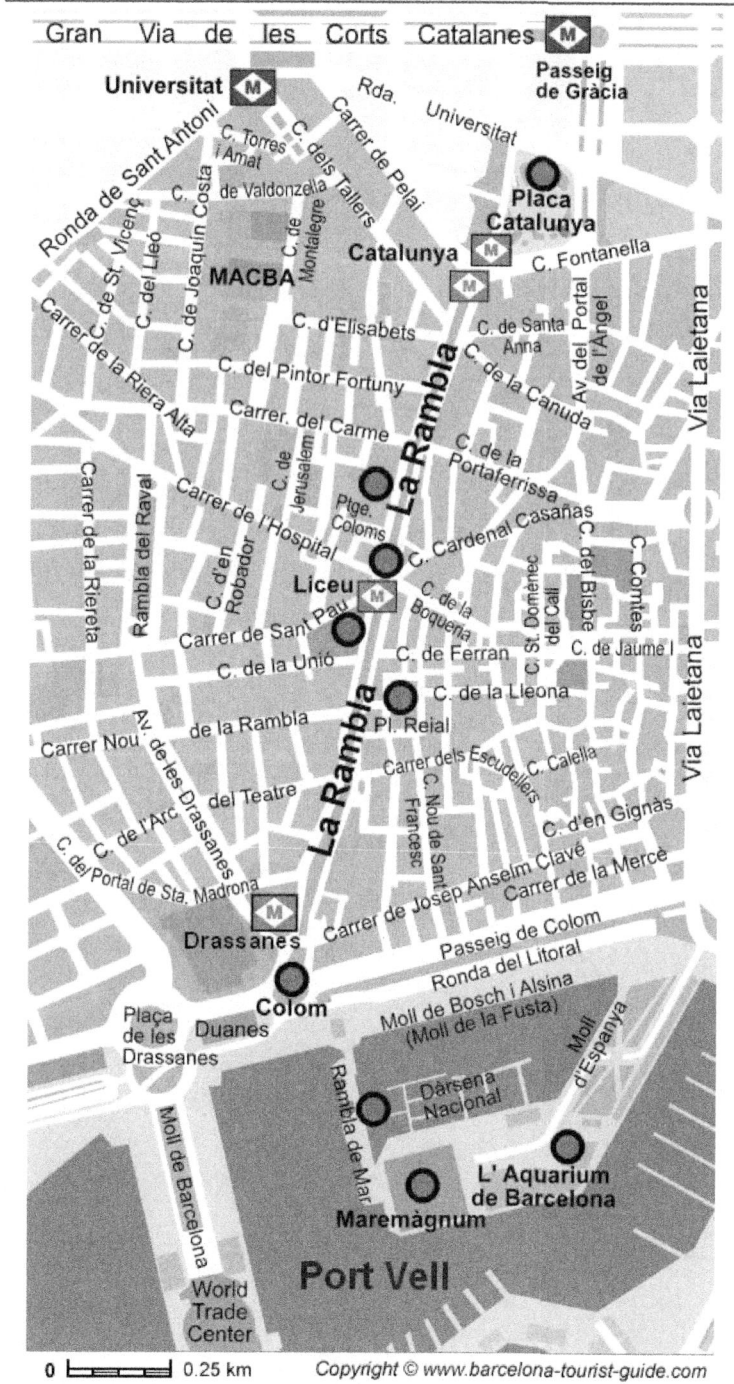

MAP 8: BARCELONA TOP 20 DESTINATIONS

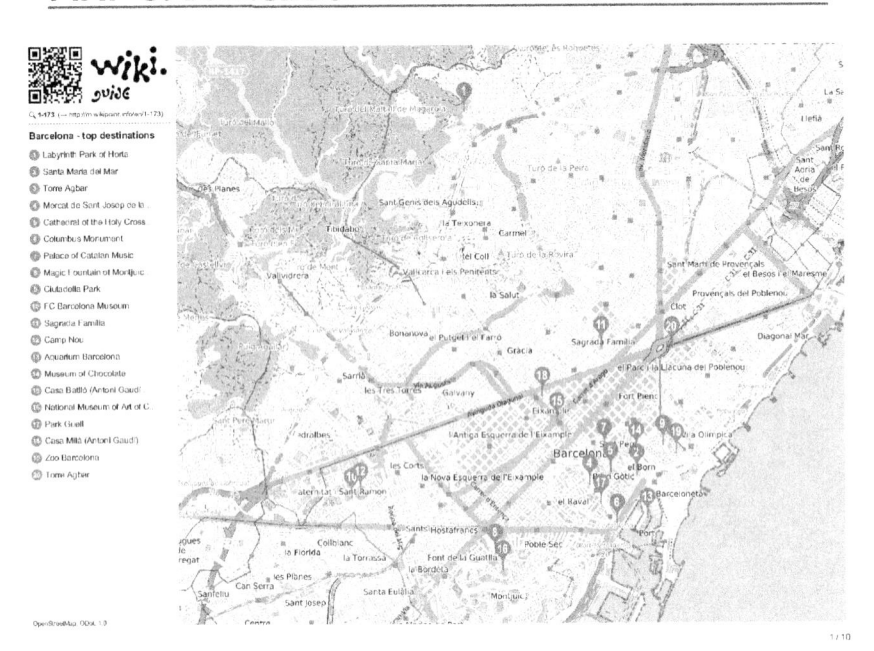

Barcelona - top destinations
1. Labyrinth Park of Horta
2. Santa Maria del Mar
3. Torre Agbar
4. Mercat de Sant Josep de la ...
5. Cathedral of the Holy Cross
6. Columbus Monument
7. Palace of Catalan Music
8. Magic Fountain of Montjuïc
9. Ciutadella Park
10. FC Barcelona Museum
11. Sagrada Família
12. Camp Nou
13. Aquarium Barcelona
14. Museum of Chocolate
15. Casa Batlló (Antoni Gaudí)
16. National Museum of Art of C...
17. Park Güell
18. Casa Milà (Antoni Gaudí)
19. Zoo Barcelona
20. Torre Agbar

MAP 9: BARCELONA TRAMWAY MAP

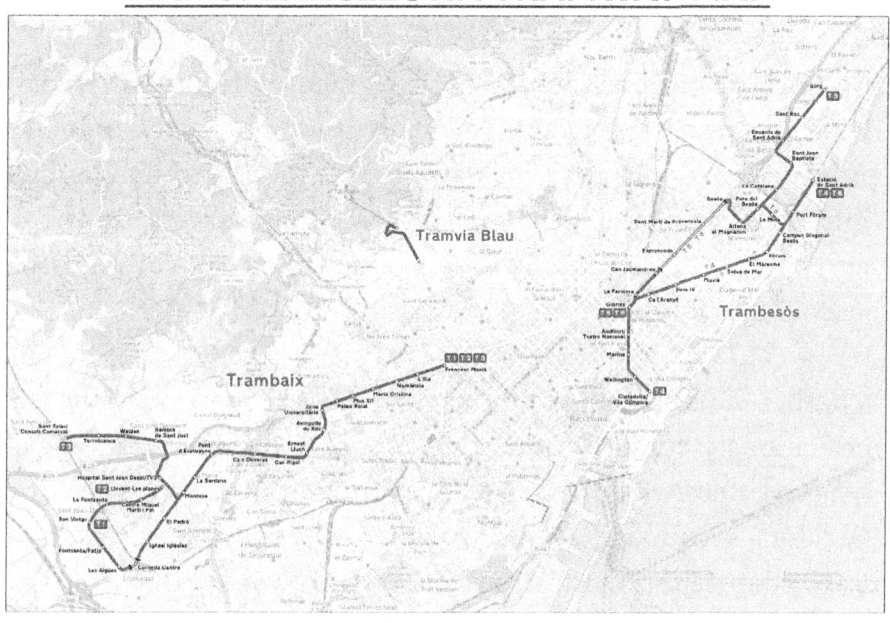

CONLUSION

In conclusion, Barcelona is a city of boundless beauty, rich history, and vibrant culture, and this comprehensive guide has endeavored to capture its essence. From the iconic Sagrada Familia to the hidden gems tucked away in its streets, this book serves as your passport to a captivating journey through the heart of Catalonia.

Whether you're a first-time traveler or a seasoned explorer, our meticulously curated itineraries, practical resources, and local insights offer invaluable assistance for planning your adventure. Barcelona's culinary scene, nightlife, shopping districts, and nearby day trips provide a multifaceted experience that caters to every traveler's preferences.

As you immerse yourself in the colorful tapestry of this remarkable city, remember that Barcelona is not just a destination; it's an unforgettable encounter with history, art, and the warm embrace of Catalan hospitality. Use this guide to unlock the secrets of Barcelona, and let its magic and allure leave an indelible mark on your heart. Barcelona beckons, and this book is your trusted companion on an unforgettable journey.

Printed in Great Britain
by Amazon